Opportunity Dubai

Making A Fortune In The Middle East

By Peter Cooper

HARRIMAN HOUSE LTD

3A Penns Road
Petersfield
Hampshire
GU32 2EW
GREAT BRITAIN
Tel: +44 (0)1730 233870
Fax: +44 (0)1730 233880
Email: enquiries@harriman-house.com
Website: www.harriman-house.com

First published in Great Britain in 2008
Copyright © Harriman House Ltd
The right of Peter Cooper to be identified as the author has been asserted
in accordance with the Copyright, Design and Patents Act 1988.

978-1-905641-97-0

British Library Cataloguing in Publication Data
A CIP catalogue record for this book can be obtained from the British Library.
We have done our utmost to contact all the necessary copyright holders prior to publication for all
photos and press clippings that are not owned by the author.

Printed and bound in Great Britain by Biddles Ltd, Kings Lynn, Norfolk

---

For Svetlana

About the Author

Oxford University educated financial journalist Peter Cooper found himself made redundant by Emap plc in London in the mid-1990s and decided to rebuild his career in Dubai as launch editor of the pioneering magazine *Gulf Business*. He returned briefly to London in 1999 to complete his first book, a history of the Bovis construction group.

Then in 2000 he went back to Dubai to become an Internet entrepreneur, just as the dotcom market crashed. He stumbled across the opportunity to become a partner in www.ameinfo.com which later became the Middle East's leading English language business news website.

Over the course of the next seven years he had a ringside seat as editor-in-chief writing about the remarkable transformation of Dubai into a global business and financial hub city. At the same time www.ameinfo.com prospered and was sold in 1996 to Emap plc for $27 million, completing the career circle back to where it began a decade earlier, and leaving Peter Cooper a multimillionaire.

He remains a lively commentator and columnist as a freelance journalist based in Dubai, and travels extensively each summer with his wife Svetlana. His financial blog www.arabianmoney.net is attracting increasing attention with its focus on investment in gold and silver as a means of prospering during a time of great consumer price inflation and asset price deflation.

Acknowledgements

It would have been nice to mention everybody who has helped me make a success of business and investments in Dubai since the year 2000, but I doubt the narrative would then have been more than a long list of names. You know who you are and please accept this apology and acknowledgement.

Even reading the proofs of the text brought back a few forgotten memories. How my old friend Simon Fielder suggested going back to HSBC to resolve my 'missing equity' problem, for example, and I had left this crucial piece of advice out of my account.

But I suppose the real stars of the show have to be my former business partners Klaus Lovgreen and Lars Nielsen whose original dot-com enterprise I was able to merge with my own ambitions to create a financial news service.

Of course I would never have moved to Dubai in 1996 without first being made redundant by Emap plc and then hired by that Dubai publishing dynamo Ian Fairservice. And I would not have joined AME Info and benefited from the subsequent sale back to Emap plc if I had not been fired by Ian.

Then again without the remarkable transformation of Dubai under the leadership of His Highness Sheikh Mohammed bin Rashid Al Maktoum, none of us would have got very far in business.

Thanks are also due to Stephen Eckett and his colleagues at Harriman House for asking me to write a book about investing in the Middle East and then agreeing to publish this one which is as much an autobiography.

Contents

1
The Eureka Moment

'Financial website sold for $50 million' read the headline in the *Australian Financial Review*. I took another sip of coffee and looked up from my breakfast around the restaurant of the modest but modern Sydney hotel. That was the Eureka moment. Surely nobody in Dubai would yet have done such a thing? There I sat, as the former founding editor of the *Gulf Business* magazine, with a new opportunity staring me in the face. The answer was obvious: return to Dubai, establish a financial portal, sell it and pick up a large cheque. All the best business plans can be written in a single line!

To explain the background to this insight, the immediate stimulus for this interest in a new business plan came from an imminent dinner engagement. I was on a trip around the world after completing my first book and that night planned to meet Phil Horan, a multimillionaire Australian entrepreneur with a very successful track record in the Gulf. I had helped to promote his business since 1996 when I arrived in Melbourne on the second Emirates flight from Dubai. It occurred to me that telling Phil I was wondering the world because I could not think what to do was not a very impressive state of affairs, so I had opened the *Australian Financial Review* hoping to find a better explanation, and the story about the financial website just leapt off the page.

But this was really interesting. I could instantly see a new and potentially highly profitable opportunity. My alter mater *Gulf*

Business had been the first new magazine published in Dubai in a decade in when it began in 1996, and had demonstrated a huge untapped appetite for business information in the region. The Internet was the media of the future though, as I had belatedly realised while booking hotels for my trip and while researching possible investment ideas in the summer of 1999. In fact with my book about the history of the Bovis construction company written and delivered I had spent a couple of months in The City analysing ways to invest my small capital. This sum I had amassed partly through a few years working in Dubai, but mainly by selling out of UK property in 1998 (far too early as it turned out). The conclusion I had reached while sitting in a borrowed apartment in The Barbican, high above City of London, was that dotcom stocks – the investment vehicles of the Internet companies – were horrendously overvalued and due for a crash.

While stock market over exuberance was one thing, the basic Internet company business model still held good promise. There was the potential to capture a large, new client base around the world, and to do it with a technology that could undercut the cost of any old economy competitor. In my own sphere of journalism the thing that impressed me most was that Internet news was always ahead of the newspapers, which had to go to press the night before and then distribute across the land. The Internet had a natural technological advantage, however low your budget and however big your "old technology" rival. But how on earth could you possibly execute such an idea as a financial portal without securing huge investment? Indeed, how much money would you need? How would you find the right staff in Dubai? This was enough to stop me after the fifth coffee. Seeing Phil Horan for dinner seemed like a good place to start.

We met in a restaurant in a converted warehouse building down by the Rocks, where the first British ships landed in Sydney harbour. Phil was his usual lively, intelligent and well focused self, and explained his latest project – another restaurant overlooking the famous harbour to be called Xertes, which he hoped to franchise in the Gulf. I mentioned the concept of going into Internet publishing and there was a glint of interest in his eye. He was keen to meet up if I returned to Dubai in the New Year. I did not tell him at the time that our meeting that evening was not merely stimulating, but was the actual stimulus that produced my big idea.

In the meantime, my 1999 world tour continued onto the Northern Territories and the Great Barrier Reef. In Cairns I registered five domain names at an Internet café before boarding a four-day diving boat cruise. These domains included www.businessarabia.com and www.buyindubai.com. Hong Kong, where I stayed with an old friend who works for HSBC, was next on my schedule after Australia, and while there I bought a couple of books on how to set up a business. Hong Kong has a strong can-do entrepreneurial ethos, but was still suffering from the post-Asian financial crisis with property prices down by 50% from the 1997 handover boom. This crisis had been forecast by one local financial commentator, and his life had been recorded in a book that I had discovered and bought from www.amazon.com. I decided to go and see the legendary Dr Marc Faber and request an interview.

Dr Doom, as he is still known to his friends and admirers, worked from a crowded and poorly lit office whose annual overheads of $1 million were so high that he was soon to move to Thailand. I found him a little touchy and difficult to pin down, but agreed with everything he had to say – most notably when his eyes rolled to the ceiling at the mention of dotcom valuations. Considering this, it was perhaps churlish to ask him what he thought about a new financial portal, but I did so anyway. He was not entirely dismissive, noting that the best time to start a business was in a recession because if it worked then you would clearly do extremely well in an upturn. Yet, true to form, Dr Doom could not see a lot to be positive about.

He would later, in early 2000, deliver some spectacularly accurate calls on the dangers of US equity overvaluation and dotcoms (see Chapter 8). He also became my first expert columnist on the website, adding hugely to its credibility. In the long run he raised his own business profile in the Middle East considerably, as AME Info ended up becoming the largest English language media in the region with an audience bigger than the BBC or CNN. In fact, CNN eventually used us as a promotional platform, but that is jumping a long way ahead in this story.

While travelling on the metro one day in Hong Kong I chanced to meet Chris, a former colleague from Motivate Publishing who had run off with Mel, the best looking girl from the office. He was now editing a local trade magazine and she was a sub-editor on the *South China Morning Post*. Chris and Mel lived on Lantau Island, a kind of hippy community for non-conformist expatriates reached via ferry. We dined under the stars on Lantau and once again the story of a future dotcom website sounded much better than dwelling on the dubious delights of being an unemployed author and 40 year old drifter. A couple of beers later, and encouraged by their reaction, I took the ferry back to stay at my old friend's comfortable apartment in the Mid-levels.

We discussed my business plan more seriously over a rather expensive meal and bottle of wine at the famous China Club (which as I recall used to be the Bank of China before undergoing a sympathetic conversion to a gentleman's club). These days businessmen and women are welcome. The Chinese food there is excellent, although it is often hard to work out exactly what you are eating and perhaps best not to ask. I am sure that by the final glass of cognac at the bar the whole small business plan was perfectly formed, and the next day I went out and bought a book *How to Write a Business Plan*. Things began to look more daunting then, with a list of one hundred searching questions to ponder before even considering the starting of a new enterprise. There was also a grim reminder about how many new businesses fail within a year.

From Hong Kong the British Airways' Oneworld ticket took me onwards to Thailand. Chris and Mel had put me in touch with another former Motivate colleague called Tom who lived in Bangkok with his lovely Thai wife. I best remembered Tom for having vanished overnight from Motivate and Dubai without a word. It was only thanks to the remarkable coincidence of bumping into Chris on the Hong Kong metro that I had located him. But Tom was extremely friendly and insisted I went to stay at his home when the three days I had booked in a remarkably under priced hotel were up. This was, it should be remembered, the time of the post-Asian financial crisis and a great time for bargain basement rooms in Asia. My five-star hotel room came in at around $40 per night.

I hardly needed to benefit from cheap accommodation by staying with another friend, but the companionship and local insight were obviously useful. Part of the reason for Tom's sudden evacuation to Bangkok had clearly been his engaging Thai lady friend, a restaurant owner he had met while reviewing her establishment in Muscat. They lived in a villa complex some distance outside the centre in a very comfortable, modern home owned by his wife. The home was complete with visiting relatives, the child of a cousin and two servants. The cooking was superb, and worthy of a former Muscat restaurant owner, but so smelly that the kitchen was outside the back door of the house.

Tom was running his own public relations business in Bangkok, and I think apart from feeling a little nostalgic for England he was also hoping for a few client introductions from the Gulf. I certainly welcomed his hospitality, which extended to a couple of nights on the town in Bangkok with his male friends and visiting some of the nightclubs filled with hostesses. In one of them a bar girl blew fire into the air as her party piece, and a drunken PR colleague decided to show how he could do it as well. He blew an enormous fireball down the bar but when we turned around his face was also on fire! A cold towel put it out and he was rushed away to casualty, thankfully not seriously injured. As a journalist I have known PR persons go to many lengths to attract attention but this is the only time anybody went so far as to set themselves on fire. We repaired back to the house before anything else happened.

I talked to Tom a lot about the life of an entrepreneur in a foreign land. It seemed his domestic circumstances were good, but business was not exactly booming. Clients were hard to come by, payments usually late and instead of employing people he did most of the work himself, often working late into the night. Nonetheless, I was impressed by the intensity of his approach and thought it sounded a successful formula, if not exactly a path to instant millions. At the same time, his standard of living was enviable and he was a good deal happier than he had been in Dubai living in a small company flat. We later visited the plot of land where he planned to build a weekend retreat, completing the neo-colonial lifestyle. It was a long way from a shared flat in Dubai.

To escape the noise and pollution of Bangkok I disappeared for a week to Railay Beach, a stunningly beautiful place off the southern coast of Thailand reached by small boats from Krabi. This region was used in the film *The Beach* starring Leonardo DiCaprio, and has jungle clad cliffs facing a pristine beachfront. Railay Beach as a resort is comprised of typical Thai beach huts available for inexpensive rental with a couple of restaurants serving Thai food, an Internet café, amazing golden sands and a crystal clear aquamarine coloured sea.

Most people do not go to Railay Beach to write a dotcom business plan but that was my objective. The beach hut was reminiscent of the simplicity of Vincent van Gogh's room in Arles – just a bed, table and an extremely basic en-suite bathroom as a modern addition. There was not even air conditioning, and I could just about see the beach from the terrace where I could write on a simple table. I thumbed the business plan guide I had bought in Hong Kong, and found the list of one hundred questions to answer before even considering starting a new business. I began by tackling these.

There was not much to distract my attention from the problems at hand, aside from a Scandinavian girl who occasionally bounced past my line of vision. Sadly I have never got on very well with Swedish girls, so I got on instead with the business plan. I found the concept fairly straightforward to outline, my costing of staff and premises were a bit vague, but I had absolutely no idea about what was involved in launching a dotcom from either a technical or expenses point of view. That evening I went to the bar, a little despondent, perhaps hoping to meet the lady from Scandinavia under more social circumstances. Instead I sat next to a small guy in glasses, and decided to open a conversation with the unlikely gambit, 'I don't suppose you know how to start an Internet company?'

Remarkably he did, and was actually on a long holiday after completing his third dotcom start-up. I immediately asked him if I could buy him dinner that night, and in return I got a very informative crash course in dotcoms for beginners. Yip – for this was his name – said that only one in a hundred succeeded, and that was in the good times. His last dotcom project had been a website that allowed you to create your own business cards online and have them mailed to you. I later used it to produce my own business cards for my new, unincorporated and unlicensed entity Arabian Internet, and everybody commented on how professional they looked.

However, much of what Yip had to say was unintelligible to an amateur like me and what I really learnt was that finding somebody like him would be absolutely essential to succeeding with a dotcom venture. But the bad news was that he was already clearly an expensive commodity and in scarce supply, and now more interested in rock climbing in Thailand than setting up a website in Dubai.

Still, it was instructive to meet the genuine article, a dotcom person, and the biggest downside appeared to be the huge number of hours of hard work needed to make a new venture succeed, provided the business idea was sound. The money looked good if you could get that far.

From Thailand my round-the-world ticket took me back to Dubai where I had not stepped foot since September 1998 when I had left Motivate Publishing under something of a cloud, although not in the middle of the night like Tom. Not to put too fine a point on it I was sacked after issuing a memo criticising a member of staff for not doing his job properly, admittedly after being warned not to write such memos. It was a sudden exit but perhaps a predictable clash with the volatile founder of the company (and famous Gulf expatriate multi-millionaire) Ian Fairservice. Maybe subconsciously this is what I was hoping would happen. Yet having to leave a newly furnished apartment after just a couple of months, and return to the UK in a hurry, was not much fun – especially as Ian conceded that I had done 'a very, very good job' as editor of *Gulf Business*. I think he liked to turn over his staff to keep costs down and egos under control.

So I was not quite sure what kind of reception I would receive on my return to Dubai after this involuntary absence. However, my old friend and a contributor to *Gulf Business* magazine, Nigel Truscott, a bright young partner in a local law firm, had kindly agreed to let me stay in his spare bedroom. He and his charming Polish wife Eva proved extremely hospitable and their very pleasant expatriate lifestyle just added appeal to the idea of coming back to Dubai to live and start a business. Nigel generously suggested that I stay on a while longer and complete the business plan. It was extremely useful to have some input from a lawyer at this early stage and Nigel appeared happy to act as an eminence grise to my new project. Eva also said to me, 'It is a wonderful idea, you must do it!' Such encouragement counts for a lot when an idea is the only asset on the table, and Nigel could offer sound practical advice from his experience of helping other entrepreneurs to set up in Dubai.

We went out diving one day with his friend John who he had helped to establish a business refurbishing old Omani chests and other antique bric-a-brac. John lived alone in a large Jumeirah villa, surrounded by stacks of chests waiting for refurbishment and had recently parted from an Eastern European lady, so was in need of cheering up. It seemed he partly blamed the demands of his business for this personal problem. In his view persistence and determination were the two characteristics that marked out a successful entrepreneur. But he was at something of a low-ebb and felt that too much relied on him as an individual. In fact, this was a common complaint among Dubai entrepreneurs and indeed managers. Too much always landed on the desk of the man at the top (and it usually was a man in those days) with others loath to accept responsibility.

John's own business model was a tough one. He employed several dozen Indian craftsmen directly from the subcontinent, and had to manage their work on a daily basis. Maintaining standards of quality with a low-paid workforce was not an easy task, but it was crucial in order that the business could succeed, and John certainly had succeeded. As it turned out a year or so later, Nigel became a sleeping partner in his business and the structure was reorganised to give him more time to himself. Apparently it worked out well for both parties.

In the meantime, while Nigel and Eva were at work during the day, I was able to use their computer to complete my business plan and go off to visit my old business friends, colleagues and contacts to consult them about my big idea. There are a few meetings which stand out. Peter Nankervis, then the head of equities for HSBC in Dubai, liked the business plan and appreciated the value of information in such an emerging market. It should be remembered that dotcom stocks were very highly valued in late 1999 and anything connected with this world had an intrinsic appeal to almost anyone in business or the financial sector. Even Nigel's legal firm had formed an ad hoc committee to consider how to benefit from the Internet. For those lucky enough to get in and out within the right timeframe this appeared to be a passport to dotcom millions, and the dotcom crash was then still six months away.

Peter Nankervis said he would introduce me to his friend David Price who had his own private equity company, Redwood Partners, owned in partnership with David Knights – unbeknown to me this company soon to be bought out by HSBC Middle East. The specialty of Redwood Partners was the acquisition of equity stakes in dynamic young companies and then selling them on after a period of rapid expansion. Unfortunately they were not interested in funding venture capital start-ups, only in buying equity in existing companies at a certain stage of development, and so my entreaties for a sum of $2 million to fund a business information website fell on deaf ears.

All the same, David Price is an excellent analyst and business consultant and a kindly, if pointedly blunt, individual. He told me I did not have a business plan, it was just a concept paper and that it would need a lot more work. He said cash flow projections would be needed and asked how you could establish an estimate of the likely revenue stream. But the clear message was that this project was too young and underdeveloped for him to be interested, though he might be interested later on if things developed further. I was amazed that somebody could be so open to new ideas and yet so closed to taking them forward.

This lunch provoked a dual reaction. First, I was annoyed to be dismissed for having just a concept paper, as my career record was one of solid achievements and not chasing after moonbeams. If I saw an idea that I thought would work, it certainly would work, and I would make it work. Self-confidence, arrogance or experience, I suppose you could take your pick, any entrepreneur needs a little of all three. Secondly, I paused for thought over the capital required for the venture. Was not the whole beauty of Internet technology that you could reach huge numbers of people for a low cost and did not really need more than a personal computer to get going? If it was really so brilliant then having a lot of money was not necessary. It might even be a burden on the future of the business that could be avoided. Capital, after all, always has to be returned sooner or later, usually with interest at the very least.

I wondered about the high capitalisation of some dotcom companies. All they seemed to be doing was raising money from investors and then spending it, without necessarily creating a viable business that had any hope of a long-term future. This looked like an investment "con-trick" more than anything else, with everybody always looking to sell out to the greater fool. And yet, as with all the best "con-tricks", there was actually something genuine that made the whole thing look attractive. The Internet was a revolutionary technology, no doubt about it, and publishing content was its raison d'être. Content was what I knew about from a decade and a half in the publishing industry and so there was a business opportunity here.

Could there be some alternative to raising cash against selling shares like a typical dotcom? If this technology was so cheap and so productive could it not operate on very tight margins and generate its own working capital? I reviewed the business plan again and again, and began looking at how tightly the business could be run, assuming that no capital was raised. What if there was no million dollar backer like Mr Price, could I do it on my own?

It is at this point in a venture that you have to think hard about what your own capabilities are worth. I was lucky in being a veteran journalist and editor with an ability to knock out words at a speed that few could match, and with enough insight and perception to command an audience. Having worked alongside sales men and women in the publishing industry for many years, I was perhaps overconfident in feeling that I could sell advertising and sponsorship to commercial clients.

The sticking point, aside from not having a trading license, office nor a company, was surely the Internet technology itself. My basic mastery of the computer could hardly be described as more than adequate. Moreover, the Internet technology skills of a true webmaster would be expensive and hard to obtain in an emerging market like Dubai. It would take a lot more than buying dinner for another Yip. Mentally I filed this point under the heading challenges and kept optimistically looking at the bigger picture.

This bigger picture came from my long experience of Dubai, which dated from March 1996 when I landed late at night in the airport and first met my new colleagues from Motivate Publishing. I had been recruited in London to edit the Middle East's first new magazine for ten years, to be called *Gulf Business*. The owners gave me an ambitious brief to be someway between *The Economist* and *Forbes* magazine. *Gulf Business* was a roaring success from day one, hardly surprising really as Dubai was in one of its periodic boom phases, the oil price was high, and we had no competition. The editorial product had also won praise locally and established my name with the business and financial community. This was a background I would need to draw upon heavily to have any hope of making a success of a financial website project.

As previously explained I had left Motivate Publishing in rather a hurry in September 1998 after a disagreement with the owner, having survived rather longer than the average independently minded Motivate editor. This actually proved an auspicious time to depart as the Asian Financial Crisis was still working its way through the global economy and oil prices dipped below $10 a barrel in 1999. In Dubai this produced a significant slowdown in new project launches and a $500 million theme park by the Creek was cancelled. Many local publishers lost money that year and it was not a very good time to be in that line of business.

Nonetheless, the predictions of an imminent real estate crash made in 1998 turned out to be very wide of the mark. In Sydney in

1999, aside from Phil Horan, I also hooked up with Colin Nethercoat, the former HSBC head of PR who had left Dubai in the belief that a real estate crash was imminent. But what had looked like an impending oversupply of commercial and residential property was easily absorbed in 2000 and 2001. Landlords sat on empty property rather than accept lower rents, and by May 2000 when I next wanted to find an apartment the rents had recovered. It was only by bribing a doorman in a popular block with a bottle of Black Label scotch that I found the two-bedroom, two-bathroom apartment I wanted in Satwa on the Mediterranean-style boulevard, Al Diyafa Street.

On the other hand, my strong feeling in early 2000 was that the timing for the launch of a new business could not be better as local business was still rebounding from the stock market crash of the previous year, and business launch costs were as low as they would go. My second reason for wanting to launch an Internet business in particular was somewhat contrarian. I strongly believed that the dotcom boom was about to go spectacularly bust just like Marc Faber was predicting, and indeed it did.

When I interviewed one bright young UAE national who told me how much money he was making on Internet stocks, and was considering becoming a full-time day trader, this only confirmed my opinion that recession was imminent (incidentally today he is the chief executive officer of a listed company and so bounced back from his Internet losses). Here lay an opportunity because, as Marc Faber said, the best time to start any business is at the bottom of a recession, for if you can make it work in the bad times then it will just have to succeed in the good times. The art is to ensure that your cost base is low enough to secure your survival under any market circumstances until the good time comes.

The wind was also blowing in this direction. In November 1999 the then Crown Prince of Dubai, General Sheikh Mohammed bin Rashid Al Maktoum, announced the formation of the Dubai

Internet City, to be up and running within one year. The original aim of the DIC was to capture some of the dotcom launch capital and bring it to Dubai for investment in a purpose built business park. Dubai was a little late in jumping on the dotcom bandwagon, and in typical Dubai fashion largely reinvented the project as a business park for IT companies in the subsequent year. However, there were a few success stories that came out of the DIC, and its first spin-off the Dubai Media City. AME Info would be among them.

Some early local market entrants were spectacularly well capitalised. Arabia.com was backed by the Saudi multi-billionaire Prince Al Waleed bin Talal, who I had featured on the cover of the first edition of the *Gulf Business* magazine. But the dotcom business model was a perverse one. You raised money and spent it, hoping that in the process you would establish a profitable, stand alone business with a slice of the Internet action. The problem was that having that cash in your hand from day one meant that the founders felt that they had already made a business success, when in fact they had nothing except a stream of business expenses. In the case of Arabia.com, it eventually closed five years later and lost $24 million, a contrast to AMEInfo.com which accumulated a similar net worth over that period. Sometimes starting poor is an advantage over starting rich.

2

Meeting Klaus And Lars

About halfway through March 2000 Nigel Truscott, my good friend and unpaid legal adviser, turned to me and said: 'You do realise that the summer is now coming up and you have not really got anything yet, have you?' That was true enough. I had been a little distracted by a business proposal from Phil Horan for a 3-D e-shopping mall which had now fallen flat. There had been a long wait for an opportunity to doorstep the local retail billionaire Majid Al Futtaim who expressed some interest in a virtual shopping mall but not enough to keep this sort of project alive.

Phil had introduced the enigmatic Majid to the concept of multiplex cinemas and even an indoor ski-slope for his shopping malls. Indeed, he did include a $150 million real snow ski-slope in his Mall of the Emirates which opened in September 2005. But the idea of the 3D e-shopping mall he rightly saw as too difficult to implement in the UAE, and in fact it flopped overseas as well. The dotcom boom was now at its height and the enthusiasm for new technology was getting a little out of hand with some pretty daft ideas being floated.

So my thoughts returned to the original eureka idea of the financial website, first conceived over breakfast in Sydney. On the other hand, I also realised that I knew very few people in the IT and Internet world in Dubai, despite several months of research. How on earth could this deficit in market contacts be made good quickly?

Then I saw an article in *Gulf News* that mentioned something called First Tuesday, a new networking evening being run in London for would-be IT entrepreneurs that was wildly popular at the time. Could something like this not be useful in Dubai too?

Nigel liked the idea. His legal practice work was slower in 2000 and he was in marketing mode looking to drum up business. Perhaps a networking evening would also produce a few e-clients for his legal practice and his senior partner quickly agreed to jointly organise it. This proposal doubtless appeared on the agenda of the regular internal meetings that Nigel's firm was holding at the time to try to tap the power of the Internet. What we did next was to think of everyone we knew in the IT and Internet sector, and invite them along for a drinks party after work, asking at the same time if they could recommend anyone else we should include. Seeing imitation as the sincerest form of flattery, we dubbed the event Last Wednesday, which was just as well as unbeknown to us the First Tuesday was weeks away from its own launch in Dubai. We beat them to it, and the first event was held in the bar of the Aviation Club.

Nothing like this had been done before and, the Internet being the buzzword of the moment, the initial turnout was promising with the bar completely full. Lars Nielsen and Klaus Lovgreen had been recommended to me by Elizabeth Gilmore-Jones from Standard Chartered as 'the only people who know anything about the Internet in Dubai' and more worryingly, 'they already have a business website that does some of the things you are talking about'. I was delighted to see them standing at the bar when I arrived and went over to say 'hello'.

It immediately proved a meeting of minds and I did not finish speaking to Lars and Klaus until past midnight. I could tell instantly that these were, as Elizabeth suggested, by far the best people to be working with. Klaus seemed devilishly clever with technology like the guy Yip I had met in Thailand, and Lars was obviously a natural salesman. He was astonishingly revealing about their business, telling me that they had made a profit of $180,000 in 1999. At a time when almost all Internet companies were competing to make the biggest losses and spend the most money, this struck me like a bolt from the blue. These guys not only knew about the Internet but could also make money from it, and seemed very straightforward and honest people. This impressed me deeply and I allowed Nigel to do most of the networking that night.

A couple of days later we picked up our discussions over lunch in the Boardwalk Café, part of the Dubai Creek Golf & Yacht Club. After thinking about their comments and actually visiting their website, which was not that impressive and pretty basic, I suggested a deal in which I would take a 10% stake in AME Info in return for joining them as editor-in-chief to develop news and feature content for the website. It seemed a perfect synergy: the Internet platform and sales energy combined with some original news and feature content to win readers and enhance the prestige of the website.

Both Lars and Klaus liked the concept. They realised that my background from *Gulf Business* and journalistic career were assets that would be hard to better in Dubai where good freelance journalists were tough to find. But Klaus baulked at the notion of an immediate 10% stake in the business, which had recently been valued at $20 million by one expert, and instead proposed a joint-venture structure with a vague understanding that this could be converted into an equity holding at some future date if all worked according to plan. I think he was sceptical about whether my idea of selling sponsorships against news and features pages would actually work. It had not been done before in Dubai, or elsewhere as it turned out.

I liked the concept of selling sponsorships rather than advertising banners though. The whole point of sponsorship is that clients sponsor a position on a page for a longer period than with advertising, typically six months or a year. For this they get a discount on the cost of comparable advertising, but crucially the website gets its money paid in advance and secures its cash flow in advance of expenses. Indeed, this revenue stream is inherently more stable than advertising which can fluctuate wildly, and sure enough did just this on AME Info after events like 9/11 and the second Gulf war. The other major advantage of selling sponsorship rather than advertising is that it takes almost the same effort to sell a high cost sponsorship as a much smaller advertisement. So this is an efficient use of time, especially if you are also responsible for the content of the website and are very short of time to sell.

Initially I rejected Klaus' offer of a joint venture partnership because it fell short of an equity commitment, but then talked it over with Nigel. Ever the pragmatist he argued along the lines of, 'well what other options do you have?' Kindly, he also said he would be happy to look over a joint venture agreement if I came up with one. That was not difficult as Phil Horan and I had got as far as drafting such an agreement between us for the 3-D e-shopping mall, so I adapted that document and Nigel corrected some details.

I think this attention to legal documents somewhat threw Lars and Klaus who were more used to informal deals on a handshake. In fact it probably slowed down the launch of our venture, which became known as AME Info FN, FN being short for financial news. Even so, having a legal document of some kind became a blessing as the enterprise grew and even more so later on when it came to crystallising the promised equity stake. Whether this was actually a legal partnership hardly mattered, and I doubt it would have stood up in a court of law. This document defined our objectives, responsibilities, ownership share and the sharing of profits. At this time I also registered my own company in the DIC, Arabian Internet, so that I was a legal entity that could do business in Dubai and form such a joint venture.

The DIC itself was so new that the buildings were still under construction, and the business license conveniently gave the right to trade anywhere in Dubai while the expense of an actual office was avoided. That meant I could work legally from my bedroom under the sponsorship of my own company. Yet again Dubai was proving its worth in allowing something to happen that would have been impossible in the recent past: namely the registration of a start-up company on a very low capital base, and the publishing of information as business type. For until the DIC was created in the autumn of 1999 obtaining publishing licenses was very difficult, and when I launched *Gulf Business* for Motivate Publishing in May 1996 this was the first new magazine for a decade, and even then we launched without the license fully in place on a nod from officials that it was coming.

Dubai likes to be a business facilitator, but I was lucky to be in the right place at the right time with the right idea. I was fortunate because Dubai's Crown Prince, General Sheikh Mohammed bin Rashid Al Maktoum, had only (somewhat belatedly in view of the coming 2000 dotcom crash) established the DIC to court the Internet boom in 1999, just prior to my arrival back in Dubai. This project not only allowed me to get going in business on my own, with 100% ownership of a company, but also created the sort of community and interest required to get a business started. With my limited resources I would not have got anything like as far as I did without the help and support of the DIC, particularly in the early days.

I can recall walking into the DIC's temporary offices in the Crowne Plaza on the Sheikh Zayed Road because there was no response to my email request for help. The intelligent young lady official who came out to assist me was the same one I had met in the Dubai Press Club a month earlier. She had moved onto the next Dubai Government project and so had I. Then there was a three minute presentation to the chief executive Saeed Al Muntafiq, now a major figure in the Dubai Government administration, a quick flash of my bank statement proving sufficient capital and that was it. For at that time the Dubai Government clearly had a policy of very loose regulation of entrepreneurs, realising that in order to find business princes it might be necessary to embrace a few frogs.

Few people understand just how alone an entrepreneur with a new business venture can actually find themselves. Unless you are a complete fool you do not discuss a good idea with anybody, and you cannot give away anything more than is absolutely essential to anyone. Therefore you are in a very lonely situation. I was very lucky in having a friend and lawyer prepared to offer help me on a pro bono basis like Nigel, and his advice proved immensely valuable. But it was obvious that this was a passing phase, and that Nigel would soon find himself wrapped up in other responsibilities and unable to provide a helping hand to an entrepreneur in need. Fortunately my new business partners had been working together for a couple of years already and could help me with this experience. Previously I had always been employed by companies with back-up staff to do things. Now if the computer went wrong I had to sort it out, albeit with Klaus on the end of the phone to help me, and that was pretty important for a new Internet business.

Not having to pay for an office proved highly beneficial, both from a cash flow and a lifestyle perspective. Keeping expenses to an absolute minimum is essential for a young business. You just never know how long it will be until your first payments come in, or what disasters will befall you in the meantime. It was also very practical to jump out of bed to do the news early in the morning without having to face a long journey to the office. Some people probably could not manage the self-discipline to work like that from home, but then setting up in business requires a discipline that only a few possess – that is why most people are probably best advised to stay working for somebody else.

You also need to have a fair cash balance, or access to funds, as the cash flow of any start-up business is usually miserably small and late, and if you mismatch expenses and income in business you go bankrupt. In my case the proceeds from the sale of two houses in the UK in 1998 left me in a comfortable situation, and the business did eventually succeed. However, it was still not until the end of 2000 that the first, small cheque was paid into my account, and by the end of 2001 my savings were down by 50% from 1999 due to the necessity of subsidising my income.

If there is one single reason why I did not give up in the subsequent two years it was probably because I could not afford to after committing all this cash. It took four years of successful trading to recoup this initial start-up investment. Yet that was a good record judging from many accounts of business start-ups. This is not something for the faint of heart or anyone without means. The joke was that if you wanted to make a small fortune on the Internet then it was best to start with a large one, and many businesses were not that successful.

But to return to Lars and Klaus: they at least had an office of sorts near to the Maktoum Bridge. It was not an imposing place for a start-up, with a scruffy old carpet and furniture from the 1970s, but incredibly cheap. Klaus visited from his home in Abu Dhabi on Tuesdays and Wednesdays and sat at a desk facing Lars, while a stressed looking Filipina secretary had a desk in the main office and doubled as a receptionist. This was the original AME Info team of three, plus their new joint venture partner. Lars' wife Anne joined a little later to update the press release content on the website and the Filipina did not last much longer.

To step back in time, Klaus had originally founded AME Info back in 1993 in Abu Dhabi, with a national business partner, to import frozen chickens from Denmark, and registered the website www.ameinfo.com in 1996. A mathematics graduate, Klaus had long been fascinated by data management and this led him to develop what was then a very innovative product, a CD-ROM business directory for the UAE. He had met fellow Dane Lars Nielsen who was then selling foodstuffs to regional supermarkets for a giant Danish company in 1997. Lars and Klaus hit it off, personally and professionally, and I think Lars immediately saw business potential in Klaus' technology skills. Finding sponsors for a CD-ROM product was hard going though, and they had come close to selling a major stake to Motivate Publishing in 1998. Indeed, I can dimly remember seeing them in the Motivate offices at that time and wondering what they were doing there, although I had no clue about their business then. Motivate's founder Ian Fairservice is one of the most successful UK expatriates in the Gulf, but he missed out on acquiring AME Info in the earliest of days. We never found out why he turned them down. His senior managers strongly supported the acquisition but were overruled.

Of course, even when the CD-ROM migrated onto the Internet website in 1999 AME Info was just a fraction of the regional information resource that it later became. The website offered no more than a search for company addresses, a list of upcoming events and the latest press releases, and in terms of sponsors and advertisers the young company was really struggling to generate any interest. What was AME Info? Who used AME Info? How could a website possibly compete with print? These were questions frequently asked and not easy to answer. The local market was very ignorant about new media, and patience and a sense of humour went a long way in overcoming the daily uphill struggle.

However, our morale was always high and I suppose Lars is a natural optimist, albeit one with his feet fastened firmly to the ground. Klaus's visits formed the highlight of the week, around which our business meetings were usually structured. Most meetings comprised AME Info or FN presentations to win new clients. There were a great many more meetings than client wins. Both Klaus and I found this a tough schedule, but Lars could be on his tenth meeting of the day and still manage to sound as though it was the first time he had ever delivered an AME Info presentation. Our long time supporter, PR and marketing consultant, Eileen Wallis once described Lars as 'the most energetic businessman in Dubai' and few would argue with that judgment.

Perhaps an early error that we later corrected was trying to squeeze too much information into our presentations, with too many marketing options for the clients to absorb. After a while you could see their eyes begin to go round in circles as Lars or Klaus would present yet another brilliant and cheap form of Internet marketing. The problem was that without a PhD in Internet technology this could appear bafflingly complex, and in the multicultural melting pot of Dubai such fellow spirits were thin on the ground. In fact, Klaus already had a following among the techies of Dubai. There just were not many of them and their managements seldom listened.

All the same the business started to come in, slowly, for FN, our financial news and features joint venture. The first solid order was from Oracle, and I took the mobile phone call from their then marketing lady, the aforementioned Eileen Wallis, as we headed into a meeting with Credit Suisse. The bank also decided to support us with a weekly column, so that was a very good day. With hindsight I know now that Oracle was just starting a fierce campaign to shift its business almost entirely onto the Internet, and I think Credit Suisse also saw the opportunity to reach new potential customers and knew me from *Gulf Business* days. Additionally I managed to swing a barter deal for air tickets from Lufthansa in return for a sponsorship. But three deals were just not enough to launch even a skeleton news service with me writing all the news.

Another sponsor that had eluded our early entreaties was HSBC, somewhat disappointingly given my previous links from *Gulf Business* days and my friend in Hong Kong. So I split up my summer holiday in 2000 and returned to Dubai at the start of a very hot August to chase up the PR and sponsorship manager Steve Martin. One of the few benefits of the summer for business is that people have more time on their hands, and fortunately that was indeed the right time to catch Steve Martin whose arm was finally twisted over a beer on a hot night out. I am sure it came down to him being impressed by my persistence rather than enthusiasm for the Internet (of which he never really seemed a fan). Again, my previous friendship with the bank from the first days of *Gulf Business* greatly assisted my case, as did my friend in the bank's headquarters in Hong Kong, who had introduced me to Steve in the first instance. Contacts led to more contacts and business.

Then in early September I was finally granted an audience with Boutros Boutros. Not the one-time head of the United Nations, but the well-connected PR and sponsorship manager at Emirates Airline, Dubai's only international brand in the year 2000. Boutros listened carefully to my plans and thought that if we gave Emirates a free sponsorship for six weeks then he might be able to get his boss Mike Simon to pay for it. Sadly that did not actually happen, but we took the unpaid sponsorship period to try it out. And although Emirates later became the biggest client of AME Info for Internet advertising campaigns, I never saw a cent in sponsorship money and had to be happy with occasional upgrades to Business Class from Boutros. Only after we had sold AME Info did Emirates finally become a sponsor.

With these five prestigious clients we decided to get on and launch the FN financial news service. Staffing was clearly an issue. There was only myself as editor, reporter and tea maker, working out of my second bedroom with a dial-up Internet connection. I saw no point in paying out more for an ISDN line, and wanted to see the Net in the same way as our average customer. Making a virtue out of necessity is a vital part of being an entrepreneur. I had no staff, so the most productive way to approach the news was to serve up a digest of the news-in-brief, not much more than bullet points of three sentences each summarising the news of the day. That much I could manage on my own. And it looked like a news bureau that specialised in briefs.

For Internet users, news in brief is easier to read than longer stories and does not involve a lot of clicking to reach new pages – click-through was frustratingly slow in those days before broadband became common. The source material for news writing is also widely available, mainly from the press releases already published on the AME Info website, but also from newspaper and agency reports which were credited as necessary. There is no copyright on news. The only downside was that this news service needed to be done early in the morning so that executives would have fresh news online when they got to their desks in the morning. I therefore began the working day at 7.30am.

When we started I reasoned that within a year we would be thriving and able to employ other journalists to do this laborious task, knocking out twenty to forty news briefs. In fact four years later I was still doing it myself, plus the original features for the website, and selling the sponsorship space with Lars and Klaus. Success does not always come easily and it took years before we had the surplus revenues on AME Info FN to employ people. I used to meet the journalists and editors from more established newspapers and agencies and envy their working conditions. They doubtless thought I must have been having an easy time on my own.

Why did we stick it out all that time? Well, being your own boss does have its advantages. You can organise your time and holidays to suit yourself, and I did manage to pay a freelancer to write the news during the quiet summer period to allow for decent holidays (see Chapter 10). But then I needed the holidays. We also had a firm aim in view with our equity prospects and the valuations achieved by Internet companies in 1999-2000 were a target to aim for, if not an entirely realistic one. Furthermore, the Internet was something new and exciting and being in a new media had its attractions.

It could be very wearying, however. There were just so many presentations, so many promises and so many letdowns. But Lars and Klaus had decided before they met me to make a policy of always being pleasant and never getting annoyed with people. I learned what this meant early on when I got upset with a business proposal refusal from Cisco. Lars and Klaus said this was just not the way they did things and I either changed or it was over. The days of editorial ego were plainly finished and I needed a cool commercial head or I was dead. It is a rational and not emotional approach to business that works well under most circumstances.

This approach paid off in the long run, and in some most unexpected ways. It might be recalled that Standard Chartered Bank was the original inspiration for the idea of sponsored content on AME Info. In fact this was one of my initial suggestions to Klaus that intrigued him when we first met: 'What do you mean you could get companies to pay to put their own content on AME Info?' Yes, that was exactly it, although they would get their own access button on the navigation bar, four advertising banners and a logo in the section, so this was pretty heavy branding and not just paid-for advertorial.

By November 2000, Standard Chartered was still avoiding my calls and ignoring my emails, but invited me to an e-commerce symposium. It was in an evening slot and I was feeling tired and yet still desperate to get the bank's business. I asked the attractive conference organiser where to find Elizabeth Gilmore-Jones but the good lady had given me the slip again, and I stayed behind to meet the bank officials. The twist in this tale is that a little over a year later I was married to the conference organiser, Svetlana, who Elizabeth described as having 'brains and beauty'. It still took another three years to persuade the bank to sponsor a column, but eventually they took on a very tenacious and ambitious young economist, Daniel Hannah, who wanted to see his own column on AME Info and persuaded the bank to pay for it.

It was a strange turn of fate that I met my wife in the second month of the FN business start-up, as the FN section had finally gone live in October 2000. I was really immensely overstretched but

I suppose I was taking such a positive approach to life that it rubbed off in an entirely different direction. Svetlana changed my life, and at 40 I had practically given up hope that the right woman would come along – she did though, and at the right time. I found having a partner in my personal life even more helpful than having business partners. For as previously noted being an entrepreneur is a lonely game, particularly to begin with, and having a close confidante is a source of personal stability as well as a reason to not give up. Looking back I am just amazed that the two life changing events could be conducted simultaneously and can only conclude that doing things you enjoy takes less effort than normal life.

3
Darkest Days For Dubai
And AME Info

No new enterprise is an entirely smooth ride from start-up to final sale. My mother warned me that establishing a business generally took longer and cost more than you expected, but the final result was often a little better than your forecasts. This homily turned out to be only too true with AME Info.

Even at the end of the second year I was still subsidising my income, having earned exactly zero in the year 2000. I had thought our financial affairs were just about to turn the corner when along came 9/11 and the terrorist attacks on the twin towers of the World Trade Center in New York in 2001. I watched the events on CNN with considerable alarm and then telephoned my old friend Peter Nankervis at HSBC who immediately realised this was big news. At first it looked like it might be some sort of a horrendous accident but not when a second plane slammed into the twin towers.

Later in the day I was sitting in the bar at the Irish Village, a pub hidden under the Dubai Tennis stadium, having a coke with my former Motivate Publishing colleague Brian Scudder. He was just about to launch the first issue of *Time Out Dubai*, and we both wondered what the terrible events of that day would mean for our projects and the Middle East in general. My reckoning was that the US would strike back immediately and hard wherever it could, and that would not be good for tourism in Dubai or advertising in magazines or on websites. I felt pretty pessimistic about the immediate outlook, especially for anybody living in a cave in Afghanistan where the US military was bound to strike.

However, there was a more immediate problem. AME Info was just a few weeks away from its debut financial conference, unfortunately entitled The First GCC Inward Investment Forum, a joint venture with the global conference giant IIR Holdings, with a Saudi prince as our star guest. Should we cancel or go ahead? We hated the idea of cancelling and so heroically decided that the show must go on.

Holding a conference on inward investment was bound to be a disaster. No foreigner in their right mind would consider putting money into a region from where terrorists had just successfully bombed the US financial capital. Citibank actually removed the tens of billions it had deposited in Bahrain after 9/11, replacing the money some months later. It made every foreign business in the region think about what they were doing here, and created an atmosphere bordering on panic for some.

The Inward Investment Forum certainly represented the lowest point of AME Info from my perspective. This had been my big idea and the event was designed to put AME Info on the map with top government officials, multinationals and bankers. The first impact of 9/11 was on attendance. Nobody even wanted to fly in the immediate aftermath of 9/11, and therefore many delegates and speakers cancelled. Naturally the subject also looked farcical in the short-term, and US banks in the region came under internal pressure with suspicions about the channelling of the funding for terrorism running wild. Some of these suspicions were of course entirely justified.

On the first day of the conference the chief executive officer of Citibank was in the chair and walked out at midday, leaving me as chairman for the afternoon session. I can only think he had a great deal on his mind, but this was unusually bad behaviour from a senior banker. It got worse. The conference star, the Saudi prince, was taken ill in the middle of the night and ended up in the local casualty ward. Gamely he managed to put in an appearance the next day, but looking considerably the worse for wear. Then the new hotel's lights failed during Dr Marc Faber's presentation, and this super professional continued to deliver his speech in pitch darkness for about 20 minutes. I will never forget his booming and confident voice in the pitch darkness, although mercifully his overhead projector continued to function.

By that time the conference organiser Shelia Mullinger had assumed the almost glacial expression of a true heroine, and was slumped on a chair in the corridor smoking a cigarette. Maybe we should have cancelled for the benefit of poor Sheila's nerves, but strangely enough we benefited in the long run from having carried on regardless and several of the participants became good friends. This included the dynamic Lale Ansingh, founder of Rawaj Strategic Communications whose husband Floris, chairman of Shell in Saudi Arabia, spoke at the event. We also broke even financially, which was definitely a credit to IRR Holdings and its tight management.

But we never got involved in organising a conference again, although we were happy to collaborate with media cash and barter deals to promote thousands of future conferences and events. Perhaps we were spreading ourselves too thinly in thinking that we could be conference promoters as well as website entrepreneurs with such a small team. However, there is a good synergy between conferences and a news website and we continued to work with IIR Holdings for many years. Without the events of 9/11 it could have been a very different experience all round.

Another dark period came in early 2002, not long after the awful nightmare of the inward investment conference. Advertising was just picking up after the 9/11 hiatus, which cost us perhaps six months in lost development time when we could least afford it. In fact, the conclusion of the 9/11 debacle from our perspective was the ending of the Afghan War coverage on television and the newspapers. To mark this occasion my old colleague Nick Rufford from *The Sunday Times* came to stay with us on his way home from five weeks reporting from Kabul. His baggage stank from sleeping in the back of a lorry to avoid stray gunfire, and Nick had distinguished himself by being able to sleep at a time when any sane journalist suffered from insomnia. We took Nick to the beach at the Ritz-Carlton, where the lady from *The Times* that he brought with him was staying, and had the place virtually to ourselves. Nick and the media circus had cleared the Dubai beaches of tourists. I am not sure my fiancé was sorry to see him go, and once the incessant negative reporting from Afghanistan had stopped, the tourists returned to Dubai and the advertising agencies began booking space again.

Life has to go on even under the most challenging of circumstances, and January 2002 was also the date we had set for our wedding. The problem was that not everyone was terribly keen on flying, and particularly not to the Middle East in that post 9/11 atmosphere. In truth only my mother, stepfather Alan and one old friend from England, Ken Hanson, seemed up for the journey. That seemed unfair on Svetlana and so we reluctantly decided to keep the wedding just for local friends. In any event, mounting a large party was just not realistic in view of the recent battering 9/11 had given my already shaky finances, and I was very glad indeed when my poor (well not so poor) mother asked if I would accept the honeymoon as her wedding present. That solved one problem, and for the reception somebody suggested that having a caterer at home had worked for their wedding. We thought it could work for us too.

However, the week before the wedding my wife was scheduled to change her residency visit because she had just moved jobs from Standard Chartered Bank to DaimlerChrysler. This process required her to leave the country and return to pick up the new visa, an anachronistic practice now discontinued in lieu of an additional fee. Somehow Kish Island, a free zone off the mainland of the People's Republic of Iran became the destination for this visa run. It was not a good choice and nobody from DaimlerChrysler ever went there again to change a visa.

Soon after her arrival my future wife phoned in deep distress as the promised visa was not ready and so she would have to stay longer on Kish Island. I gathered the hotel was horrible and that she did not feel very safe. Also, they had supplied her with Islamic dress on arrival. At first I thought it sounded a bit exaggerated and tried to calm her down, but later in the day I was at a press conference at the Burj Al Arab and took a second call. Svetlana was most upset and said the wedding would have to be cancelled and that I ought to come and rescue her. As I was at a press conference I naturally asked the PR lady what she thought I should do, and Susan Furness rose boldly to the challenge telling me, 'You go to Kish Island and I will rearrange the wedding. What about 14 February, that's a romantic day for it?'

So I got in a taxi to go to the airport, and Susan instantly became best woman and attended to the wedding arrangements. I landed in Kish Island after a half-hour trip on an old British Aerospace 1-11 aircraft of a vintage I had not seen since being a package tourist to Spain as a child, and bowled up to Iranian immigration. I could see a couple of Pakistani workers being given a hard time by an over-inflated Revolutionary Guard and tried to look confident but not arrogant. He asked why I wanted to visit Kish Island, and I responded, 'Tourism and relaxation, I hear it's a very nice place!' The guard beckoned me through with a smile, and said 'Have a good stay!'

The heroic part of saving my wife consisted of locating her at the only five-star hotel where I had suggested she should go and wait for my arrival. She had by then bought her own Islamic outfit, not liking the immigration authorities' choice. It was just as well nobody asked for a marriage license when I booked into the hotel, and we had dinner and walked around the pathetic Kish Island the next morning. Thankfully it was not long before we heard the good news that the visa was ready and we promptly flew home. The only tourists we saw in Kish seemed to be fellow unfortunate visa run victims stuck through no fault of their own. It was not so surprising really. There is no alcohol on Kish Island, the hotel swimming pools have been emptied and women have to remain fully covered on the beach or when swimming. The breakfast and dinner at our five-star hotel included the same feta cheese salad and bread, unforgivable really as the Iranian food we eat in Dubai is delicious. And as for local attractions there was a peculiar complex of mud caves and a hopeless duty-free shop selling the cheapest Chinese goods.

The actual wedding went off very well, Susan had performed wonders and the caterers, vicar and friends all rallied round. I still felt sorry that a terrorist attack had kept our family and friends away, but it was clearly most important to actually have a bride in the country. Sadly the change of dates meant that Lars and Klaus could not make the big day as they were in Kuwait on business. We drank a toast to absent friends and that included them. But there was another challenge lurking in the shadows which proved a more enduring headache.

Lars and Klaus had been introduced to a former BBC television presenter called Timothy Blythe who was now running a local TV channel. Mr Blythe was trying to drum up support for his own great idea, a new business TV channel to be based in Dubai. Years later he did in fact get to launch a channel for somebody else which made quite a splash, although he parted company with the channel not long afterwards.

Lars and Klaus took Blythe very much at face value, and before I knew it he was being touted as a fourth partner in AME Info, if things went according to plan. What the full business plan was and what this really involved remained obscure. Klaus always liked vague deals that left maximum room for manoeuvre and I wonder if Blythe had any appreciation of the real value of structure and equity in a business venture. Most likely he did not. He certainly seemed to have little notion of commercial realities or revenues, and was completely taken in by my one-man news team for which he had great plans. His vision was for me to present the news each day on a TV channel as well as write the news briefs in the early morning. I found it difficult to take this seriously and thought this all a huge waste of time and wished the guys would just concentrate on sponsorship sales and advertising.

Klaus later rationalised the whole Blythe episode as an experiment in television, seeing video as an element of Internet publishing that was going to emerge as important – he sensed an opportunity to learn about television from an expert without paying much for this consultancy. Lars, I think, initially saw more commercial value in Blythe, although he became increasingly more sceptical as time went on and eventually totally disillusioned. One of our mutual associates described Blythe as a 'fantasist' and noted that the Dubai Government was hardly likely to allow a TV news channel to launch that was outside its control, let alone advertise on it. The simple facts of business life are often the most obvious.

Eventually, Blythe's grand plan ended up perhaps as Klaus had imagined it might – just another channel on AME Info. We provided him with a free apartment from a barter deal for six months and he talked a lot of rubbish about video to our clients. In my view we should have been spending our efforts building up what we had, and not dallying with video where the Internet traffic was bound to be very low in the start-up phase. This was overly pessimistic perhaps. By the autumn Blythe could see his grand plan had failed and he took up a lucrative offer from a regional TV channel to launch an English language show that closed after six months. But he did leave behind his colleague, Lisa Creffield, who stayed with us to develop video content in an able and professional manner, and AME Info joined the video revolution with its own video channel.

Would we have been better off concentrating on the post 9/11 recovery of advertising and sponsorship rather than being distracted into the world of video? It is one way of looking at it and we could have worked on the video channel at a future date. But people with grand TV plans don't come along everyday, and Blythe could talk the hind legs off a donkey. He was a very able presenter and not bad as a TV channel managing director either. However, without a strong practical and commercial streak business ideas are just hot air. I can remember a rather lavish re-opening party in the Sheraton Hotel in late autumn 2002 at which Blythe broke the news about his new job. It was a moment to go and find another glass of champagne, and breathe a huge sigh of relief.

We had one other troubled episode in the early days of AME Info, and that was our sudden and rather rash decision to employ an Arabic editor and to launch an Arabic edition. This happened in the spring of 2001, not many months after the launch of the FN financial news section. We made two significant errors of judgment: first, that our existing clients would automatically agree to sponsor an Arabic edition and, secondly, we decided to employ an Arabic editor – at the very high salary of Dhs30,000 per month – who appeared ideally qualified and usefully could also manage our accounts.

Ismail proved a disaster all round. It was a while before we found out that the news in Arabic was running several days behind the news in English, and therefore not strictly news in the accepted sense of the word. He also managed to get the accounts in a terrific muddle which we later had to outsource, and took a chartered accountant months to unravel the mess. The worst problem of all was his large salary. Not only was this actually larger than my own take-home share of the profits but when the Arabic advertising income failed to materialise it also hit my profit share for six because I was responsible for paying 50% of Ismail's salary.

I decided to shoulder this burden as part of the cost of building up a small business, and kept my own counsel for some time. For, as a part of the FN business, this did mean that if Arabic came right then this would count towards my profit share and ultimately help determine my equity interest in the business. After six months I almost gave up my share of the Arabic website investment but had second thoughts and kept going. This was a mistake as things went from bad to worse on sales, and Ismail's performance was not improving either. Eventually, in the new year, I told Lars and Klaus that I was giving up on Arabic. They agreed and then sacked Ismail and found a lower cost alternative. This worked reasonably well, but it was still a few years before the Arabic site was an asset and not a liability to the business. Indeed, in time it contributed to the image of a universal business content service for the final sale to Emap, and we all got our investment back.

But it kept me poor for a second year in a row at AME Info, and left my personal fortunes at a nadir when the crisis of 9/11 knocked us out for about six months. It was only then that I started to earn an income comparable with my days at Motivate Publishing. And it was not until 2003 that we were doing well enough to pay out a regular salary of Dhs30,000 to myself – exactly what Ismail had been earning two years before. Mercifully that was just in time to give me enough of a salary track record to qualify for a mortgage to buy a villa in Dubai. This proved to be an excellent investment, as real estate in Dubai was initially significantly under-priced to get the market going, and it was actually a faster way to make a first million than as a partner in AME Info.

Accountancy is known in the trade as the dismal science, and many moons ago I rejected the certainty of a career as a young chartered accountant with KPMG in London to pursue my dream of being a journalist and writing for a living. But the Ismail episode was just the first of two or three major dramas concerning the AME Info accounts. It was too easy to say that with a growing business to run we became distracted and so did not pay adequate attention to the figures. We should have kept a better eye on the money. But we did not and it cost us dearly. Cutting costs in the accounting department is not something I would ever recommend in future.

Once Ismail had left us Klaus turned to a local accountancy practice run by a guy named Ron who also looked after the accounts for Barbara Saunders, our PR agent. Ron knew what he was doing and we managed to untangle the FN accounts from the rest of AME Info with only one emergency meeting with Klaus in Abu Dhabi. He also employed a very efficient Filipina lady to maintain the invoices and to collect money, and for the first time in the brief history of AME Info the bank balance began to grow as invoices actually got paid. However, this also emboldened Ron to raise his fees and we soon parted company, unable to agree on a part barter and part cash deal to promote his company's services on the website. We should have stayed with Ron, with the benefit of hindsight, and paid our fees like any other client.

Klaus moved pretty fast in finding another agency that handled accountancy on a contracted out basis, and the handover seemed pretty smooth. We just got on with building up the business, meeting prospective clients and signing up deals. It was only around six months later that we began to realise that something was going terribly wrong. In fact, as it transpired, almost zero invoices had been issued in the period. There was little point in finger pointing or recriminations in our small team. The responsibility was really a shared one, and none of us had spotted it, although I had begun to ask questions about my lack of revenue. Klaus entered one of his rare moods of ill humour, but again set about finding a way of putting right what had gone so badly wrong.

Enter Jeannette Vinke, a qualified chartered accountant with an MBA and about to quit KPMG in Dubai, who Klaus found through a recruitment agency. She quickly discovered just how badly the accountancy had gone awry under the now previous outsourcing, and recruited another young accountant, Rohini, to help sort the mess out. A great deal of work was needed to rebuild our accounting system into something worthy of the name, and to begin with this meant a lot of backdated invoicing which upset a few clients, although in the end not many refused to accept it. It was a shambles, and Jeannette later concluded that if AME Info had not been growing so fast at that particular time between 2003 and 2004 then we would probably have gone bankrupt.

As it happened the cash kept on flowing in, and in such a large quantity that we failed to notice what was up until it was too late. But a lot of items had to be written off in the 2004 accounts and this depressed our bottom line earnings for that year. To be fair I had kept the FN accounts separately and these were in better shape, so that part of the group income held up. But overall we should have done much better in 2004 than the figures show, and that was down to "an accounting oversight" as these disasters are termed.

However, the pressure on Jeannette mounted as it was in May 2004 that I had re-contacted David Price, now running HSBC Private Equity with his old partner David Knights, and we needed to be able to show audited accounts for any consideration of an investment in AME Info. But as the next chapter will show, Jeanette rose to the challenge she had been employed to overcome, and the once struggling start-up emerged from an adolescent crisis into early adulthood in a matter of a few months.

It was as though we had completed our rites of passage. The battling away to secure business began to bear fruit. Doors that we had been knocking on for years started to open, and there was a compounding effect as existing clients began to spend more and the increased activity on the website attracted new sponsors and advertisers. It was not as if Lars had gone out and changed his aftershave, but he smiled more and only groaned at the sight of the stack of paperwork needing his attention on his desk.

4

The Largest English Language
Media In The Middle East

At what stage people began to take AME Info seriously rather than view it as a mildly eccentric dotcom start-up is hard to pin down. Internet traffic figures were the first sign that AME Info was becoming a force to be recognised, and there was also a more subtle change in our reception in that we no longer had to explain who or what AME Info was. Suddenly everybody seemed to know us and was using our service.

In the early days of the business the reverse was true. I remember sitting down with one senior businessman in Arabic robes and he asked: 'Can you explain to me, just what is the Internet?' When you are trying to sell web advertising, this is not the most auspicious opening question. We had to be, and were, endlessly patient and made hundreds if not thousands of presentations to anyone who would listen.

It was actually not difficult to get people to listen to us. Most businessmen and women appreciated that the Internet was something new and exciting and might be useful to their business, if only they could get their heads around it. That was not always so easy for technophobic people. For them, talking to the guys from AME Info was easier than reading about the Internet, or in some cases actually logging on and surfing the Net. We just kept on talking and talking – Lars probably woke up talking about AME Info and only stopped when his head hit the pillow at night.

As a new type of marketing tool we also faced opposition from the entrenched old media with their interests to defend against a new rival. The advertising agencies were at first brick walls to our message. In time we could appreciate why. They had existing clients and booked advertising space annually. Then along came a new media with immediate demands that upset this careful planning. In addition, we often sold directly to their clients through our presentations, which annoyed the agencies greatly as they worried that their role as middleman would be compromised.

Looking back this represented a typical development cycle for a new business. First we were knocking on doors and getting a cool reception. But perhaps it was the only way to get taken seriously, and gradually we embraced the agencies and they embraced us, if reluctantly. Indeed, we found it much easier to work with the agencies on our side than with them trying to upset our pitches, and it soon became clear that if AME Info was to grow to a reasonable size then the agencies would have to be a big part of the picture. If nothing else a friendly agency would pitch our products to its clients and relieve our sales team. When this worked it could work well.

At the same time the major Dubai advertising agencies all caught the Internet bug, partly due to client pressure and the global dynamics of the Net, and also because advertising agencies are always sensitive to the next big thing, so they developed their own in-house Web advertising divisions. A few specialist agencies were launched as well, such as Flip Media whose dynamic founder Martin Diessner was greatly encouraged to set up on his own by Klaus and Lars who knew him from the Emirates Airline account. We did a lot of business with Flip, which later followed AME Info in securing HSBC Middle East Private Equity as a shareholder, not surprisingly on Klaus' recommendation.

To take an example of how client development progressed at AME Info let us consider Emaar Properties, Dubai's biggest listed company and real estate pioneer. We chased the ever-changing executives of the marketing department for a couple of years, making our presentations and getting nowhere. Then I discovered that Emaar had taken on a new marketing manager called Tim and went to see him quietly on my own. I suggested to Tim that Emaar could sponsor a new column called *Dubai Property* in which I would write about the benefits of buying in Dubai and comment on the developing market. Tim liked the idea and sold it to his superiors. This was a foot-in-the-door and we were delighted to learn shortly afterwards that Martin Diessner was to look after Internet promotions for Emaar. It might even be that I had recommended him for the job. We liked to look after our friends and they then looked after us.

Under the able guidance of Flip Media our new client started to appreciate the best ways to use the Internet to win new real estate business, and the results were impressive enough to reach the ears of the charismatic Emaar chairman Mohammed Alabbar. In no time we added the sponsorship of the *Real Estate News*, and by the time AME Info was sold to Emap plc, Emaar was one of our biggest clients with email and Internet advertising campaigns for each new real estate project launch. Now, I would be the first to admit that this was a case of tapping into an already growing market, but how long would it have taken us to win this business without the original sponsorship and the dynamism of Martin who could spot a web marketing opportunity several kilometres from a PC screen?

Not every sponsorship client we won turned into a major revenue source, but it was a pattern that repeated often enough to seriously impact on the bottom line. Of course, just as important was having the Internet product to sell against a growing readership. Leadership from the technological point of view was down to Klaus and his one-man development team in Abu Dhabi. There was only good old

Erik Stensgaard in Dubai to handle our computer system, although we later got some backup in Canada for Klaus, and Lala came to assist Erik. What is undeniable is that Klaus' genuine enthusiasm, hard work and acknowledged genius as a web developer were the most important reasons for the success of AME Info. What Lars and I did was more of a sideshow in comparison, although it more than paid the bills.

The development of a separate website for PDA devices, the handheld computers that become very popular with the technologically upwardly mobile at this time, is an example of Klaus in action. He appreciated that our news in-brief output would be ideal for these small-screen handheld devices, and had the program up and running in a couple of hours – in six months we had around 25,000 people a day downloading their PDA news from AME Info. It was not a huge number in Internet terms, but I began to meet people who knew us from the PDA website and had become regular users. One was an incoming chief executive officer of Standard Chartered Bank, Ray Ferguson who later booked a sponsorship package. Personally I found the PDA a fiddly and irrelevant medium, and soon abandoned the machine on my desk. The fact that it had taken me longer to learn how to use it then it took Klaus to program it for AME Info said much about our respective technical abilities.

From the editorial perspective the development of AME Info gradually gathered more and more credibility over the years. It was always a question of achieving the highest levels of productivity with the smallest resources, which at the outset meant just me as news and features writer, editor and columnist. A few old friends and former colleagues also offered to help with free contributions in the early days, and this was extremely useful.

Two of my friends from Trinity College, Oxford, Tim Lebon and Steve Toms, now a Professor of Management Studies at the University of York, kindly agreed to write columns. Meanwhile,

Wolfram Bielenstein, the former deputy head of East German state radio news and a collaborator on *Gulf Business*, established our Berlin bureau in his spare bedroom and contributed items on business links with the Gulf. Wolfram was a very loyal friend and contributed without payment for more than five years before we reluctantly decided to shut the Berlin bureau due to a frustrating lack of support from German sponsors.

It was also great to include Dr Marc Faber, the celebrated contrarian investment expert from Hong Kong, as a columnist. As explained in chapter one, I had originally met Dr Faber and interviewed him during my trip around the world in 1999, and I think he saw an opportunity to become better known as an analyst and fund manager in the wealthy Middle East. As I suspected would happen, his column soon became the best-read feature section on AME Info as his forecasts proved accurate time and again (see Chapter 8).

From Dubai we were honoured to have the talented local businessman Mishal Kanoo as a columnist for 18 months, another friend and contributor from *Gulf Business* days. Mishal is one of life's natural journalists and can write an instant opinion column on almost anything. His first concern understandably remained the multi-billion dollar family business that he oversees from Dubai, but his following among the nationals undoubtedly added to the status of fledgling venture.

Otherwise, the role of editor-in-chief of AME Info could be a solitary job, with no office and no staff. To save money on office rent I opted to work from home, and even when we could afford it this proved more practical with the news day starting at 7.30am. Avoiding a commute to the office made sense, and on many days I was sat in my pyjamas writing the news. Then I would move onto features before getting dressed to go out to press conferences and meetings. I wrote a great many words myself, some three million by the time we sold AME Info, or enough to fill around thirty novels.

All the same, AME Info was growing its staff. But the deliberate policy was to spread into as many areas of the Internet content business as possible, and not to expand the FN cost base until absolutely necessary. The unusual circumstances of the launch of the video section in 2002 are covered in the previous chapter. This represented the first addition of a journalist to our team, but we kept video journalism largely separate from the written word, and the one woman video-journalist operation already had quite a beat to cover.

On the other hand, our ex-CNBC VJ Lisa Creffield took some of the weight of interviewing off my shoulders and this was very welcome. As a member of the team she was popular with the clients and agencies and stood out as a blonde with a video camera, which kept the AME Info name in the frame. She also brought considerable enthusiasm and dedication to this media, which turned into a commercial success after a couple of years.

People often thought that AME Info was running with fifty or more staff, but we never got above twenty, and I suppose this illusion of size was maintained by our constantly moving around. Lisa and I went to a lot of press conferences, usually different ones, and I also went to endless networking events and commercial meetings. This activity created an illusion of having a lot more staff than we actually did. It might have been the case that *Gulf News* had ninety writers but normally only one person attended an event.

Each month Klaus would produce a traffic report for the website and this was emailed to our key clients. We always managed to produce some impressive numbers. But the recipients were understandably sceptical about our claims, and wondered what the big figures actually meant. In the early days there were also very few individuals working in Dubai with the specialist knowledge to comprehend our data, and I often felt that Klaus was talking mainly to himself. This was not entirely true. Ayman Abouseif, Oracle's streetwise marketing manager really understood it and used the

Internet to enormous advantage in promoting his business software. The Oracle founder Larry Ellison was an early convert to the media, and legend had it he liked to design his own web advertising campaigns. That sounded almost as hands on as Klaus.

The big turning point for our traffic data was when we decided to go for a proper media audit. I began by contacting BPA World in London and holding some exploratory meetings, but Klaus eventually opted for eABC, probably because it was a better known name in the sector. At first the results presented us with a problem as eABC stripped a lot of auto-generated traffic out of its figures that had been inflating our data, such as electronic trawling by the search engines.

However, Klaus established the reasons for the difference and we just made sure that the traffic was properly described so that nobody confused the old and new data. Armed with an eABC audit Lars could indeed convince some of the most sceptical agencies about our performance and growth. The figure for unique users was the key guide and could be compared to the circulation statistics offered by magazines or newspapers for their readership.

Our first eABC certificate showed that we had hosted 236,238 unique users for May 2005 and five months later we had 651,193, which Klaus queried as looking far too big an increase. The eABC officials appeared insulted and produced a long list of reasons validating their conclusions. 'We expected the number of users to double, rather than nearly treble,' said Klaus in a press release. 'This rate of growth is likely to be an exception rather than the rule.'

Looking back, 2005 was a peak year of the oil boom and that explained this phenomenal growth, not that it subsided quickly. By October 2006 AME Info could boast 801,468 unique users, with 853,166 in March 2007. To put the 853,166 users into context, you have to consider that the leading regional newspaper, *Gulf News*, has just over 100,000 audited readers and that few audited magazines can break the 30,000 circulation barrier. Certainly in the English language media of the Middle East there was nothing approaching the AME Info platform in terms of size of audience. Even BBC World and CNN International could not match the figures. AME Info had become the largest English language media in the Middle East by quite a wide margin.

What on earth was attracting so many readers? It would be nice to think it was the quality of the editorial product, but the detailed breakdown of the viewing figures that Klaus shared with us privately did not support this conclusion. In fact it was the constant publishing of daily press releases on the website that drew in the hundreds of thousands of users. That much was clear from the data we collected for individual sections of the website. Even the news digest service, with its forty to fifty news briefs a day, never got much beyond 15% of the total traffic, and as time went on the Arabic edition of AME Info topped even that modest achievement.

Why did people want to read press releases on AME Info? Yes Anne-Birte Stensgaard and her team did a good job checking and posting the information. But the real trick was in the timing. Readers came to appreciate that press releases were posted very quickly on AME Info, and generally appeared the day before they appeared in the other media, so it was the best place to go for news information. It was just like the old days of newspapers and the scoop. AME Info was first with the news.

Klaus also did a first-class job as webmaster in making this huge flow of information accessible and keeping it organised. On a typical day AME Info might publish well over a hundred articles and the archive ran into the hundreds of thousands of items. Having this information at your fingertips in the fastest time possible was clearly crucial to the success of the website.

This often came down to the Google optimisation process. Klaus spotted the importance of search engines in general early on, and

Google in particular. He re-wrote the entire code of the website from scratch to optimise AME Info for Google, and this made sure that AME Info articles appeared at the top of most Internet searches on business subjects in the Middle East. It was hugely important in securing AME Info in the hearts and minds of Internet users, and undoubtedly the best marketing tool for a new website. But how many webmasters could write their own code? Not many in the Middle East. I can only think of one.

At the same time Klaus created the MyAME Info experience, a customised website for any user who filled out a simple registration form. This provided us with a database of regular users of the website, and it was quite clearly stated that the quid pro quo for offering MyAME Info was that users would get a limited number of paid-for email advertising messages. In return the readers also got to add sections of the website to their watch list so that they received free daily email alerts about new articles, and each registered reader could compile their own watch list to monitor whatever their preference. It was a brilliant system to generate reader loyalty and boost our traffic.

Over the years we also developed some excellent marketing barter deals which provided us with great visibility at business conferences and in other media. However, I remain convinced that none of them came close to being as important as Google, MyAME Info and the search engines in terms of marketing AME Info. Where the other media did help was in establishing our credibility with clients and agencies, especially those who did not use the Internet much themselves.

Advertising daily on CNN International was the biggest of these deals and the most effective. For once, a deal came to us. Lars answered the phone one day and it was CNN looking to see if we could help them with the launch of a website CNN Arabic, an Arabic language news site. In return for a button linking AME Info to CNN Arabic, and a large banner campaign, we got five, rising to eight, adverts a day on CNN International, with a worldwide audience estimated at 150 million.

Our own video producer shot these adverts, which CNN brilliantly later suggested should feature our own clients explaining why they used AME Info for marketing. So a $1 million TV advertising campaign cost us almost nothing and allowed us to promote the careers of our top advertisers within their companies. And CNN liked the traffic we produced for its Arabic website so much that this campaign was still running at the time of writing this book.

Our link up with IIR Holdings, the Middle East's leading conference producers, was probably almost as effective. This relationship arose partly from the disastrous joint-venture conference we held with IRR just after 9/11, which brought us closer in adversity, and perhaps alerted their bright senior executives to the power of AME Info. Nowadays, almost every conference you go to will have a media partner, usually many of them, but this was quite a novel concept back then. It was a complex package deal but basically AME Info advertised the events in exchange for a logo in the conference literature and up on the stage. As time went by AME Info was marketing a couple of thousand events a year, and similar deals were struck with other conference organisers. In fact it became so successful that we began to offer part barter and part cash deals, and actually made money out of it.

Another neat marketing initiative was to have our roll-up banners displayed at the Dubai International Airport in a position where anybody arriving or leaving the airport had to pass our them. It certainly impressed clients and agencies and demoralised our rivals. Klaus asked me one day 'How can we get our banners in the airport?' I thought for a moment and said I would go and interview the head of PR and marketing and see how that went.

It was not long before I was in the office of the glamorous Anita Mehra Homayoun who started as a young graduate at the then small Dubai airport and was now in a senior position in a much bigger airport. At the end of the interview I mentioned our idea about putting banners up in the airport. Lars and Klaus went to see her the following week and our banners went up in exchange for an advertising campaign on AME Info. Others also tried the same pitch but Anita charged heavily for the next banner advertisers.

The Dubai media was growing wildly at this time with new magazines launching on almost a weekly basis, and Lars would often swap a few adverts with the excited owners whose publications often closed within six months. More enduring was the outdoor advertising media which Lars and Klaus courted energetically. We ended up with a huge roadside display for right opposite the exit from Sheikh Zayed Road into the Dubai Media City, and a fleet of six buses painted in the AME Info black livery which plied the main business routes of the city. We only paid the cost of the materials used. The rest was a barter deal.

Perhaps our final marketing coup was the signage on the side of our office building in the Dubai Media City (DMC). Lars and Klaus pestered the officials in charge of the DMC remorselessly until we had a neon sign on both sides of the building. Considering that we occupied only one small office, which later expanded to two units, this was a clever move that made us look bigger than we really were, and impressed the advertising agencies surrounding this building as well as our future owners Emap plc.

Just to step back a little, the fit-out of our offices in the DMC was another example of bartering our product to fulfil a pressing need. In 2002 we were committed to taking up new premises in the DMC free zone under the terms of our trading license, and this presented our young company with a problem as cash resources were running low at that time. Klaus asked, 'What do you think we should do?' and I replied, 'Well who are the best fit-out specialists you can think of?' He said 'Kinnarps of Sweden'.

I found the Kinnarps website and conveniently the managing director's personal email address was listed. I wrote to him suggesting that if he wanted Kinnarps to become the best known fit-out company in the Middle East I could ensure that it happened for nothing more than the cost of fitting out our new office. Remarkably he replied straightaway and we met his team in Dubai the next day and got our fine new offices, not for free but at a huge discount. Many visitors used to admire our beautiful, minimalist offices and probably thought we must be doing well to afford them.

If this description of AME Info's growth makes it sound more like a series of opportunistic moves linked by technology than a business plan then that is admittedly true, and perhaps most successful businesses only look well planned with the benefit of hindsight. The reality is that business changes constantly, and flexibility and adaptability to circumstances are essential to survival. Yet there had been a big idea, and our motto 'The ultimate Middle East business resource' – was close to being a mission statement as well as being a pretentious objective.

Therefore when ex-Dubai Radio disc jockey Phil Blizzard sent Klaus an email suggesting that AME Info set up an Internet radio station this came within the general plan, even if it was an idea that was not on the agenda at that point. In typical fashion Klaus quickly researched the technology, and having mastered Internet video there was nothing in radio technology that could faze him. But in this instance it was definitely a case of finding the right man, and not just the logic of adding a business radio station to AME Info.

We, all of us, immediately fell for Phil Blizzard the radio personality, who is a throwback to the 1970s Dave Lee Travis and Noel Edmunds type of DJ, and much loved in Dubai. In truth we could also see the marketing potential of having Phil Blizzard wandering the corridors of the media waffling about AME Info, and interviewing the great and good. He also did produce a pretty cool radio show, and soon mastered the digital media single-handed, exactly the kind of high productivity that made the Internet profitable, and took a stab at selling radio advertising with some success.

Phil and Klaus raced ahead with developing Net radio for AME Info, and one day I was caught unaware when a young female journalist phoned and inquired of me, 'Can you comment on AME Info getting into podcasting?' I had not a clue what podcasting entailed but referred the caller back to Klaus as 'the only person qualified to comment'. As I found out, podcasting allowed all of AME Info's audio content, from celebrity interviews to product reviews, business features and travel guides, to be downloaded onto an MP3 player and listened to offline.

'It's perfect for users working in offices where noise is an issue, or for those who want to listen to AME Info's range of audio features on their drive home,' DJ Phil explained in a press release. 'We give our users full control: all AME Info features are free to download, and there is no restrictive copy protection, so AME Info podcasts can easily be shared with friends and colleagues, or listened to over and over again.'

The podcasting term came from Apple's iPod. But any digital audio player or computer with the appropriate software can play podcasts. And unlike radio or streaming media, podcasts are time-shifted, meaning that listeners have control over when they hear the recording rather like a VCR playing back a pre-recorded TV show. This meant that AME Info audio features are always instantly available, and can be listened to at any time. So Klaus and Phil had come up with another first for the regional Internet, and that was "podcasting", something I did not know about until after it was launched on AME Info.

There came to be almost a contest between Phil and Lisa, the video producer, to capture the highest profile interview candidates. Phil would manage to corner the President of Emirates, Maurice

Flanagan for a three-part series nostalgically reminiscing on the history of the region's biggest airline, while Lisa would manage five minutes with Tiger Woods. Having famous names and faces on the website added glamour and excitement and did our growing reputation no harm at all. When Phil managed to bump into Rod Stewart on the beach for an interview one day, or when he woke Sir Richard Branson up from his slumber on a Virgin Atlantic bed I am sure some listeners noticed.

Meanwhile, I kept on attending press conferences, trade shows, conferences and evening events as best I could, considering the demands on my schedule and lack of staff. In the busy season Dubai has a bewildering array of events and the skill lay in spotting the opportunities and avoiding time-wasting.

My eye was also on commercial potential as well as editorial value. My position as editor-in-chief was uniquely well placed for cornering new potential clients – interviews in particular are a great way to meet people. Sometimes it was a matter of passing a name onto Lars, other times I would get back with a direct sponsorship proposal. Even in 2006, after AME Info was sold, I still landed Orange Business Services and the Abu Dhabi real estate companies Sorouh and Aldar from editorial meetings.

On the other hand, I would not wish to distract too much from the hard work of Lars in building up our sales. He was the power behind the editorial throne that really got the commercial work done. It was a soul-destroying struggle against huge odds. Daily the dozens of sales pitches went out through emails and endless meetings were held. The highs and lows of winning and then subsequently losing business for no good reason must have been very hard to cope with, and Lars often looked stretched. No doubt he was, especially as the volume of business grew and grew. But companies would constantly book, then cancel and delay huge campaigns. Lars also faced considerable frustrations and disappointments in trying to grow an effective sales team.

Was it just that Internet advertising sales are very hard? Or did we lack the experience to manage a sales team effectively? That is a hard judgment to make even looking back, but the net result was that the sales work landed back on Lars' desk time and again. We had some successes, notably Elias, an energetic Greek from South Africa whose persuasive and persistent approach won him useful new clients.

But we had a series of business development managers that promised much, and convinced us of their worth, but then failed to pull in any meaningful revenue. Again, Lars would have their mess to clear up as well as maintaining his own portfolio of clients. Klaus and I would help out as best we could – of course maintaining Lars' morale was very much in our interests. At least he could sell the Internet, even if it seemed an impossible task for almost everyone else.

The tide eventually turned in our favour and we won backing from some unexpected quarters. In March 2006 newly elected IAA World President and leading Dubai advertising boss Joseph Ghossoub told 2,000 delegates from 67 countries attending the IAA World Congress in Dubai that the industry was in danger of falling behind current media trends and losing its relevance.

'My generation used to read books, magazines, go to the movies once a week,' he said. 'The current generation wants everything at its fingertips: WAP enabled phones, Bluetooth, SMS, video, iPods, wireless broadband, BlackBerry, podcasts and TiVo.' This was a remarkable volte-face from a man who would be the first to admit that he preferred printed media and magazines over the Internet himself. But Mr Ghossoub only became so powerful by recognising trends and he was clearly going to keep up with the times.

On the other hand, in the investment world I am what is known as a natural contrarian, somebody who likes to jump the other way to the crowd and I could not help but think that if Mr Ghossoub was now on our side then our work in developing the new media must surely be almost done. The next stage would surely mean a dozen me-too imitators and our competitive advantage and high profit margins would go to the wall.

Spotting when a business model has matured is very difficult to say the least, and perhaps being sure that you at least get out while you are on top is more than most people manage to achieve. You also always have to leave something on the table when you sell a business or you will not find a buyer – if they can then take the business to another level by infusing the benefits of a bigger group, good luck to them. Knowing your own limitations in business, as in life, is an important thing.

5
Dubai Steals The Limelight For Regional News

It is obviously true that AME Info focused on the UAE in general and Dubai in particular. This is hardly surprising as the amount of press releases generated by the UAE comfortably exceeds the output of the rest of the Gulf Cooperation Countries by quite a large margin. There is also the question of scale. Would it be interesting to concentrate too much attention on the few millions in profit generated by a small Egyptian bank on a day when Emirates spends $10 billion on new aircraft, making the front page of the *Financial Times*?

To give recognition where it is due, Anne and her team of press release ladies kept on writing to PR agencies around the region requesting additional press releases for our coverage, and this did have some considerable effect. With the oil boom of the 2000s the UAE was the epicentre of investment activity though, at first only in Dubai, but then increasingly in Abu Dhabi and also Qatar where huge gas reserves and a welcoming regime for foreign direct investment set economic growth on fire.

Given our tight resources we could only really follow the news and comment on the biggest events. We could not generate stories from thin air – something which even the strongest news factories find hard to achieve in any case. But the same-day publishing of press releases brought us many admirers on the web. We also followed up news agency exclusives with our news in brief, usually remembering to credit the source, if only to cover ourselves in case the story later proved incorrect.

Astonishingly, we also managed to sell our news in brief content back through the same news agencies which seemed unable or unwilling to do this job themselves. Over time it became quite a nice little earner, although the Reuters division Factiva had struck a hard bargain in our early days and took 80% of the revenue. We never made a great deal out of content sales and that was one reason why. Much later I renegotiated this deal to 70% which, as the Factiva negotiator pointed out, was a 50% improvement. It never seemed enough, but I suppose a lot of it was their content in the first place.

Obviously the tragic events of 9/11 were covered fully on AME Info and at the time we struggled to understand what the consequences would be for the region in our editorial, noting:

'There is only one story in the Middle East, and that is what the US response to the appalling terrorist attacks on New York and Washington is likely to be. According to the UK's *Sunday Times* the US is preparing to use ground troops, and is set to attack targets in Yemen, Lebanon and Afghanistan. The exact timing of these raids is naturally unknown, and this is speculation, but the US Government has been preparing its public for a long campaign and not a swift act of retribution. Wall Street is readying itself for a stock market crash on Monday when trading resumes for the first time since last week's horrific events. Middle East bourses are already marking down stocks sharply as business confidence has been shaken by events and sovereign debt is now virtually illiquid in the region. In this atmosphere, financial markets cannot expect to have a good week ahead and business interests are naturally very worried about the outlook.'

AME Info had its own reason for being worried by the economic fall-out from 9/11 as we were about to host the First GCC Inward Investment Forum (see Chapter 3), and it was hardly a time to be promoting foreign investment into what was about to become a war zone. We nonetheless decided that the show had to go on and continued with the conference, but the $25 billion Saudi Arabian Gas Initiative to open up the gas sector to foreign investors soon became the first economic casualty of 9/11. The hotels of the Gulf were also empty as tourists gave the region a wide berth for several months, and trade shows suffered from poor attendance.

It was a stunning announcement from Emirates Airline at the Dubai Airshow in November that started to get things moving again. The Dubai Government placed the largest order in aviation history with a heart stopping $15 billion order for Boeing and Airbus aircraft. As AME Info reported:

'Airbus officials just could not stop smiling all week as they reflected on what an order for 22 superjumbo A380s would mean for their company. Even normally sceptical commentators saw Emirates' order as a staggering declaration of confidence in the future of Dubai in particular, and the aviation industry in general. Emirates Airline chairman Sheikh Ahmed bin Saeed Al Maktoum said he was targeting 180% growth by the year 2010, and for good measure announced that a $2.5 billion third terminal will be added to Dubai International Airport over the next few years.'

The then Dubai Crown Prince General Sheikh Mohammed bin Rashid Al Maktoum was on the platform during this press announcement. It was perhaps his finest hour, and so typical of this remarkable man. He had a huge vision for expansion at a time when many folk thought the world had just ended. This vision was underpinned with solid business logic that applied the low operating costs of the A380 to Dubai's other intrinsic operational advantages and came up with a $15 billion buy order. In February 2002 Sheikh Mohammed astounded us again with a vision to create a new international financial centre in Dubai. AME Info asked, 'How practical is this idea? What does it really mean?'

'For a financial services centre to thrive – like London, Hong Kong or Singapore – the first requirement is a credible regulatory structure. It seems that the DIFC will create its own regulatory authority, doubtless modelled on successful regional examples such as Bahrain. For the UAE Central Bank has declared that the DIFC is a project for Dubai alone. This is not an impossible mandate by any means, but it will require careful implementation, and the DIFC's high-powered new advisory board will be needed for active duty. From the point of view of creating the infrastructure, the DIFC is envisaged as a dense block of skyscrapers behind the existing Emirates Towers on Sheikh Zayed Road. Nobody who has watched the speedy creation of the Dubai Internet City and the Dubai Media City can suggest that Dubai is not up to this job. But even in Dubai it will take two to three years before such a complex can be physically created.

'It is to the DIC and the DMC that we should turn to see what the DIFC will be in practice. These IT and media free zones have done a commendable task in promoting the emirate as a hub for the New Economy, and have attracted some big new names and moved a lot of old names to a new location. Expect the DIFC to offer the same attractions for international finance. A world class office complex, with current Dubai based financial firms – perhaps HSBC, Credit Suisse, ABN Amro, Citibank, the list is already quite impressive – mingling with new recruits drawn from the upper echelons of the financial world.'

This was a spectacular vision, and took time to implement, with not a few little local difficulties along the way. But once a path is set

Sheikh Mohammed rides over the problems as if he is on horseback. In the case of the Dubai International Financial Centre (DIFC) the challenges came in a clash between the hired expatriate regulators and local officials over who had the ultimate authority in determining land development strategy, and the sacking of the regulators did not go down very well in financial circles. An acceptable alternative solution was soon found though, with global investment banks taking the lead in developing the DIFC, which then immediately became a highly successful real estate project as financial institutions are the wealthiest of blue-chip tenants.

Similarly the centre's own capital market, the Dubai International Financial Exchange (DIFX), failed to get off the ground due to the unfortunate timing of its launch at the moment when the local Dubai financial market crashed. But with more than a hundred major financial institutions licensed to operate from its premises five years after the founding of the DIFC, and a massive fully-let financial zone under construction, it is surely just a matter of time before the DIFX is reinvented into something that works. However, the hubris that accompanied the launch of the DIFX, with the promise of a dozen initial public offerings in as many months, remains a blot on the DIFC's record book along with the sacking of the regulators.

The DIFC was founded just as the second Gulf war unnerved regional business for some months. As an editorial commented in early 2003:

'For travel and tourism war is bad news indeed. In the first Gulf war airlines stopped flying in the region and that kept the tourists at home, despite the obvious lack of risk in places like Dubai and Oman. Even a short, lightning war in Iraq followed by a swift regime change would have an impact on tourism this season. Alongside tourism goes retailing. In Dubai some stores obtain 25% of their business from visitors. Indeed, residents also tend to stop spending as an immediate response to a crisis. For trade shows and conferences a war is also clearly a major problem. But it will be much worse in Kuwait and Jordan, which are neighbours of Iraq. Rich residents will tend to flee at the first sign of a conflict, and not return until the shooting is over. That leaves sellers of luxury products and upmarket cars with a hole in their sales figures.'

On the other hand, our comments about the likely outcome of the second Gulf war now look hopelessly optimistic:

'Some bankers believe that a post-Saddam Hussein Middle East will swiftly settle down to be a much better place to do business. Iraq itself will open up as a massive new market, and it is to be hoped that Iran also adopts a more welcoming approach to foreign investment – and recent signs are encouraging. Perhaps with Iraq under control, the United States would then feel morally obliged to contain the excesses of its ally Israel, and provide a just settlement of the Palestinian question. Then the Middle East could begin a new era of peace and prosperity. For 2003 the IMF forecasts GDP growth of 4.7% in the Middle East, the best performance of any region in the world. Indeed, the outlook for Middle East business is more likely to be a third oil boom than a long term set back, and any upset to business will be short term.'

Well, at least the final part of our analysis was correct!

Sheikh Mohammed's vision was blessed with high oil prices and there is nothing like money to help a vision turn into reality. As AME info noted in the spring of 2003:

'This year the Opec countries have been blessed with good fortune in their efforts to control the world's oil price. First, oil prices skyrocketed upwards in the run up to the war in Iraq. Then a huge release of oil supplies, largely by Saudi Arabia, headed off the threat of emergency stockpile releases during the war itself. Thus post-war oil prices are not around $10, as after the 1991 Gulf War, but above $25. The question now is how long can it stay like this?'

For many years as it turned out. Additionally, it gradually became very clear that far from being a minus for Dubai, the aftermath of 9/11 was very positive. As one investment banker told me at the time: 'Arabian money will come back to Arabia.' So it did, with rumours of chartered Boeing 747s landing in the Kingdom stuffed with gold bars and dollar notes returning from the United States, which had become a country that no longer welcomed Arab visitors. A sheer frustration with US immigration policies, and a very real fear that assets might be frozen in error by overzealous US officials, led to a spectacular flight of capital. It also meant that as oil revenues grew there was more pressure to find a place closer to home to invest money. Why not Dubai, then, with its record of managing mega projects and creating a thriving trading city on the edge of the desert? Where better in fact?

With the benefit of hindsight it is easy enough to see where the money came from that drove regional stock markets to new record highs and funded the explosion of real estate projects that are the subject of the next two later chapters. There are no precise figures but some pretty good guesses. Repatriated money ran into the hundreds of billions of dollars, according to bankers, while the total amount of money committed to real estate investment projects soon rocketed to over one trillion dollars. The Gulf oil surplus of $500 billion in 2006 was larger than the combined trade surplus of Japan and China. It was a very good time to be the CEO of Dubai Inc. with a wealth of visionary projects to implement.

AME Info commented:

'If Dubai has got its timing right – and it looks to have got it right – then all this development will happen at a time when the Middle East is undergoing an economic transformation thanks to high oil prices. This will compound the well thought out business planning of the emirate with an economic windfall. Great cities emerge from time to time in world history, often at the epicentre of trading empires. This seems to be the destiny of Dubai.'

But Dubai had many critics at this time, and AME Info was often a lone voice defending its record. In October 2002 we mulled over an attack on Dubai by the *Financial Times*, and commented:

'Business is not about democracy and politics. Business is about making money, and Dubai has been rather better at making money than Bahrain for some time. It follows that banks and financial institutions, whose business is taking care of money, will be attracted to Dubai. The *Financial Times* this week accused the Dubai Government of obsessive secrecy and autocratic rule. This is the sort of rubbish that people write sat behind desks in London. The Dubai government is open and accessible, and about as business-friendly as it is possible to imagine. There are courts and a good system of commercial law, and a government with vision, imagination and the sheer energy to put projects into action. The *FT* is also quite wrong in claiming that the Dubai Government censors the press. This is a UAE federal matter for a start and in practice censorship is minimal.

'When bankers and financial institutions visit Dubai they see extraordinary real estate projects, a growing IT and media sector and they are confronted with the $2 billion Dubai International Financial Centre, now under construction. Dubai's ambition and its extraordinary capacity to deliver major projects cannot fail to impress, and the comparison to the years of under investment and under achievement in Bahrain is only too clear. Bahrain struck back this week, announcing plans for a $1 billion Bahrain Financial Harbour. But typically, construction is not expected to start until May next year and the development company is not even formed yet. Surely it is time for Bahrain to wake up and get its act together.'

October 2003 marked another step in the evolution of the city with the launch of the $5 billion Dubailand mixed-use theme park, the Middle Eastern answer to Disneyland, which is being built on two billion square feet of land behind the Emirates Road. This area, stretching from the back of Emirates Hills nearly as far as the Creek is almost as large as the existing area of metropolitan Dubai and the park consists of forty-five separate projects from a 'space exploration' exhibition to full-size dinosaur enclosure.

Announcing the project to the Dubai community the then Crown Prince General Mohammed bin Rashid Al Maktoum pointedly called on local businessmen not to keep their money in a bank account but to invest in Dubai. Dubailand includes the biggest shopping mall in the world, The Mall of Arabia, several new five-star hotels including one built in sand dunes, an indoor ski-slope, a complex of sports stadiums, and an ecological dome to grow vegetation in the heart of the desert.

There will also be an equestrian centre, aviation display, modern art gallery, water amusement park, multi-cultural garden complex, the largest zoo in the Middle East and some pyramids. Dubailand is designed to entertain and amuse the 15 million tourists a year Dubai intends to attract by 2015 and it will vastly add to the hospitality infrastructure of the emirate. This is to be nothing less than the leisure and entertainment hub of the Middle East, and a world-class tourism attraction similar to Disneyland in Florida.

Will the Dubailand project work? I had consultants visiting my offices on a regular basis, no doubt earning nice fees for recycling my opinions back to their employers as research. The general view was negative, but then if you had asked a consultant about building Las Vegas in the desert in the 1930s you would have got a similar raspberry. For you can only really do due diligence on an individual part of Dubailand and not on the vision of the whole thing; it is also a matter of time. How long have you got to make a project work?

If you have your own cash and a long-term perspective then this is very different to being a leveraged developer with bankers baying at your door. Dubailand was definitely pitched at the former and not the latter camp.

For a comparable project in the history of Dubai you needed to look back to the Jebel Ali Free Zone and understand what happened there. This massive, man-made port facility was the grand vision of Sheikh Mohammed's father Sheikh Rashid who decided to spend several billion dollars on what was probably the greatest single project of the late 1970s oil boom. If you adjust that cost for inflation, it is still more expensive than any single project being built in modern Dubai. When the oil boom turned to bust in the early 1980s the Jebel Ali Free Zone was created to make use of a giant port in the middle of nowhere. At first this venture looked like the biggest white elephant project in the region, but today the Free Zone is a pillar of the Dubai economy and a model widely copied around the world. That is not to say that Dubailand may not experience a few teething problems in its early years, just like the DIFC, but long-term thinking, equity investment and a bigger plan for tourism will likely produce another major asset for Dubai. Dubailand is designed above all else to ensure that visitors to Dubai choose to spend longer here on their holidays and spend more per capita – this is a part of an integrated tourism and travel development strategy that will see an enormous expansion of the Emirates Airline, the Dubai airports (there will be two of them), and the hotel sector.

At the start of 2004 one of the most widespread predictions from economists was that the oil price would fall as the year went on. True, after reaching wartime peaks of around $40 per barrel, oil prices had eased back to under $30 per barrel. The short-term reason was clear. The rehabilitation of Iraqi production was taking longer than predicted post-war due to looting, sabotage and general anarchy.

AME Info's editorial begged to differ on predictions that the oil price would fall, which came from Standard Chartered Bank among others:

'We are now told that a return to full pre-war production levels is likely by the end of the year, presumably by the same people who thought we would be back to full production by now just a few months ago. Oil is a matter of supply and demand, and when supply increases the price will fall, say the experts. Yes, but what if demand is much higher than expected and the supply side continues to disappoint? Step forward the world's fastest growing economy. China is growing faster than anyone forecast this year, and has to import oil to sustain this growth. In the past decade Chinese oil consumption has doubled to around 4.5 million barrels a day, and has to import most of its oil from the Middle East because its own resources are small. Now if China sustains its 10% plus rate of economic growth, it is not hard to see that China represents a major new source of oil demand.

'But let's not forget the Western economies. Surely the sort of fiscal and monetary stimulus applied by the US over the past year will soon produce a resumption of strong economic growth. Maybe it will be next year, rather than this year, but it certainly will happen. Then we will see oil consumption rising again. However, as we saw in the mid to late 1970s there is no reason why a bull market in commodities cannot be sustained during a period of lacklustre economic growth. Indeed, the parallels between what happened in the mid-1970s to the global economy and the situation today are very strong. A war in the Middle East followed by an oil price surge, stock market crash and sub-par economic growth. There is also the theory that under such conditions excess liquidity will find its way into commodity prices as it has nowhere else to go. Again, high oil prices will be sustained long into the future and for much longer than most economists currently believe is possible.'

This editorial optimistically concluded:

'For Gulf Oil States this is clearly extremely good news. A third great oil boom is happening right now and will last long enough to make many people extremely rich. I would argue that this position will only be reversed when there is an overinvestment in new production capacity. And after a 20-year bear market in commodities, it will be some time before investment in new capacity really gets into top gear. Hence, high oil prices will last for five years.'

In spring 2005, Emirates Airline's Chairman Sheikh Ahmed bin Saeed Al Maktoum announced a record $708 million profit for 2004/5, up 49% on the previous year. This was an amazing performance at a time when many European and US carriers were struggling to break even or under some form of bankruptcy protection. It confirmed that the Emirates' business model was superior to its rivals with lower operating costs and a booming home market. Sheikh Ahmed reiterated the Emirates' target of a fleet of 151 aircraft by 2012, and dismissed suggestions that higher fuel costs could slow this acquisition programme down. 'If anything we will be doing more, but I don't want to spoil our announcement in the autumn,' he said.

Perhaps the important point is that while rising fuel costs do hurt Emirates, the pain is also felt equally by all its competitors. So there is no competitive advantage for them, and Emirates can continue to benefit from its strong Dubai hub and lower operating costs such as non-unionised, young staff. Emirates then employed 25,000 staff so this was a very important factor. And it is this sort of long-term competitive advantage that has enabled the airline to grow from nothing in 1985 to its present size, aside from an excellent expatriate management team to support Sheikh Ahmed.

Figures released at the first annual Arabian Hotel Investment Conference in May 2005 confirmed Dubai as the city with the highest investment going into hotels per capita in the world, ahead of Las Vegas, with a commitment to build 30,000 more rooms in Dubai over the next four years. A spokesman from Deloitte pointed out that this increase was needed to meet the expected surge in demand for hotel bedrooms. In 2005 the Dubai hotel industry was red hot, with occupancy levels above 80% and room rates on the Jumeirah Beach strip at $150 per night, the highest in the region. Under these circumstances almost any hotel project looked a great investment.

Many AHIC conference speakers alluded to the global location of Dubai – straddling east and west – as a major advantage, aside from year-round sunshine. As AME Info commented:

'There was also universal admiration for the long-term vision of the emirate's ruler and its infrastructure. Nowhere is more symbolic of this phenomenon than the manmade The Palm, Jumeirah where some 37 hotels are under construction including the giant Atlantis hotel – in only a couple of years The Palm, Jumeirah will become the most famous new hotel destination in the world. Doomsayers have been predicting the end of the Dubai tourism boom for the past decade, and have always got it wrong. Today they mainly stay silent.'

At the same time, as Emirates Airline continues to buy aircraft and expand its route map, the airport facilities of Dubai have to grow. I can remember arriving in Dubai in 1996 and being told that the existing airport would increase capacity from 12 million to 25 million passengers a year within a decade. That was the logic behind a phased expansion of the airport. It looked hugely ambitious in 1996, but 10 years later and this forecast of passenger flow was actually exceeded.

Therefore, spending $4.2 billion on the new terminal three looked like a fairly good idea. But even this is not enough. Dubai is getting a completely new airport at Jebel Ali, the Al Maktoum

International Airport, coded JXB, that will be phased to allow it to grow to 120 million passengers a year, larger than any other current airport in the world. JXB will be closely linked to the seaport Jebel Ali Free Zone, creating a unique logics hub for aviation and shipping, and will become the centre of the next urban extension of Dubai, downtown Jebel Ali.

But it goes further. Meet the Dubai Aerospace Enterprise, with a projected investment of $15 billion by 2015. The business concept here is to create a new hub for aviation, from the leasing and maintenance of planes, to training personnel at a new university, to operating other airports and even manufacturing aircraft. As Sheikh Ahmed explained at its launch: 'From its base in Dubai, DAE will be uniquely positioned to drive the development of the industry forward across all markets. We have shown how much can be achieved. Emirates is one of the great airlines of the world. With the forthcoming Jebel Ali airport complex we will have the world's greatest facility.'

It clearly makes excellent business sense to lever off Emirates position as a major buyer of aircraft to promote the DAE to the aircraft manufacturers like Boeing and Airbus. Moreover, the other major airlines of the region are big customers for new planes, and will appreciate such aviation services on their doorstep. Indeed, the Middle East and North Africa region will take 58% of wide bodied aircraft deliveries between 2004 and 2023, and 50% of recent new aircraft orders have been in the Middle East as the regional carriers are in the process of doubling their fleets.

The DAE has a phased business plan to create an aviation hub at the new Jebel Ali airport complex, and has established six operational subsidiaries across fourteen industry segments. By 2015 the DAE is expected to employ 30,000 people and to have 8000 students a year passing through its university. 'This is yet another example of Dubai Inc. spotting a new business opportunity and mobilising its resources to capitalise on the opening,' commented AME Info.

By 2006, however, some of the gilt had started to come of the Dubai boom and while the Dubai Government's flagship Emirates Group continued to grow at a blistering pace in the year to end of March with revenues up by 27% to $6.6 billion and a higher passenger load factor of 76%, profits grew by a more modest 5% to $762 million. That slowdown in profits growth was attributable to higher fuel costs, yet it was also a sign that Dubai still conducted business in the same global market place as everybody else and suffered from the same problems.

'We were hit by a double whammy of higher fuel costs and increased competition,' Sheikh Ahmed told a press conference. 'Our fuel surcharges only clawed back 41% of the higher jet fuel costs which now represent 27% of the cost of flying compared with 13% five years ago. We have also faced increased competition on many routes.' All the same, over the next eight years the airline will receive an average of one new aircraft each month, and by 2010 Sheikh Ahmed said the airline will have 156 aircraft, with the Airbus A380 super jumbo leading the fleet.

Emirates remains at the forefront of Dubai's ambitions to expand its tourism to 15 million visitors a year by 2015. Sheikh Ahmed has said that the main barrier to reaching that number is the pace of hotel building in Dubai rather than the expansion of his airline. He also refutes accusations that Emirates receives hidden government support and subsidies, noting that the group's success is based on a sound and simple business model which focuses on growth and investing in innovation as well as leveraging on the natural economic advantages of Dubai as a business and tourism centre.

Yet his boss – His Highness Sheikh Mohammed – kept the ball rolling in May 2006 with another bold vision for the future, a $27 billion hotel district within the Dubailand theme park development.

Reminiscent of the themed hotels of Las Vegas and Disneyland in Orlando, Florida, the Bawadi district will add 60,000 rooms in 51 hotels to the Dubai inventory, and includes more than 1500 restaurants and bars. The centrepiece of Bawadi will be the world's largest hotel, Asia-Asia, which will have 6,500 rooms of which 5,100 will be four star and 1,400 will be five star rooms. The Asia-Asia hotel is scheduled for completion in 2012.

The stated objective is for Dubai to have 15 million tourists a year by 2015, compared with 6.2 million in 2006. This clearly requires massive growth in hotel rooms – and Bawadi will make a big contribution, although many hotels are already under development in the Emirate. Bawadi is being developed by a unit of Dubai Holding called Tatweer headed by Saeed Al Muntafiq, who has been leading the multi-billion dollar Dubailand theme park project since its inception, and has an excellent track record of delivering ambitious Dubai projects to date. A sharp reader might have spotted that the same Saeed Al Muntafiq gave this author his trade license in the year 2000, and had clearly climbed up the ranks since then.

Tatweer is to construct three themed hotels at the start, middle and end of the ten-kilometre strip. This is the classic Dubai government pattern, with the government acting as the lead investor. It is interesting that the government is taking such a large part of the investment in Bawadi for itself. Perhaps the Dubai government is almost reluctant to give up too much ownership in this lucrative sector to outside investors. Much of the sector remains under state control despite the potential for the privatisation of Emirates Airline, for example. This confidence will doubtless not be lost on potential hotel investors who have a rare opportunity to buy into the Dubai tourism sector in the Bawadi district.

Yet as 2006 came to a close the International Monetary Fund suggested that the pace of growth was bound to slacken. 'The UAE growth rate this year will be one of the fastest in the world but these rates cannot persist,' IMF regional director, Mohsin S. Khan, told a news conference. 'You will be hitting capacity constraints especially in the construction industry.' It was obvious to any observer that the city's roads could only accommodate so many construction trucks, backed up along the Emirates Road. There was a physical limit to how fast construction could be completed, and the competition for labour and materials was driving prices sky high.

As AME Info noted:

'The first thing to note about any economic boom in history is that it does not last forever. The question is rather, how long will a boom last and what will be built while it is going on, for what is built today will stand tomorrow when the boom is long gone'.

We pointed out that:

'The lion's share of new investment in infrastructure in the Middle East has gone into Dubai, with an estimated $200 billion worth of projects now underway. If you visit Abu Dhabi or Doha you see the start of a similar scale of construction activity. But it is just starting and not nearing completion, as is the case for at least $100 billion worth of projects in Dubai. Thus if something crashed energy prices tomorrow morning, and the GCC states suddenly felt their revenues shrinking, Dubai would have gained the most in terms of infrastructure.'

This article concluded:

'You just look around the city: a new airport about to finish, another bigger one about to start; massive mall projects; the tallest building in the world under construction; hundreds of residential and commercial towers going up; the three palm islands and associated projects; many new hotels being built; and Dubailand, a theme park bigger than present urban Dubai. And if we look to 2010, which is only a few years away, it is quite clear that Dubai will emerge as the most modern and sophisticated city in the GCC, if it is not already, and extend its lead over other cities which have been much slower to put development activity into place.'

So no apology is really required for having focused so much of the AME Info editorial comment on Dubai from 2000-2007. Dubai has managed to position itself to achieve the maximum inward investment advantage from the oil boom, and it is only now that other cities are belatedly getting their act together. No doubt in the late 2000s Abu Dhabi and Doha will share more fully in AME Info's editorial coverage, and in point of fact two of the most recent additions to its columns are Abu Dhabi Property and the Qatar Focus.

6

The Dubai Real Estate Boom

Nobody could miss the Dubai real estate boom of the 2000s and the popularity of AME Info site partly rode on the back of worldwide interest in the property sector. This was a period when global property markets soared on the back of US interest rate cuts after the dotcom crash and 9/11, oil prices headed up and up, and Arabs returned their money to the Middle East. But what really secured the dynamism of the Dubai real estate market was the market reform in May 2002 that allowed foreign buyers to own property for the first time ever in the UAE, the second largest Arab economy. And so there was an element of catching up with the rest of the world as well as keeping pace with a global property boom.

The crucial economic reform liberalising the Dubai property market set it on fire. Slowly at first, but with gathering momentum, buying Dubai real estate became the talk of the town, and AME Info saw an opportunity to lead in this sector with relevant comment and analysis. My own 12-year background as a construction, housing and property journalist in the UK helped considerably. This was my old area of expertise, and a chance to build on previous modest triumphs such as calling the UK housing market crash in 1991 correctly and winning a bet with the *Financial Times* construction correspondent Andrew Taylor about the downturn that year. It was an opportunity for a transfer of knowledge of a very particular kind.

At first many expatriates were extremely wary of the announcement by the then Crown Prince of Dubai, General Sheikh Mohammed bin Rashid Al Maktoum, that they would now be able to own property. There was no new law as such, just a promise by the Dubai Government and Sheikh Mohammed to guarantee these purchases until there was a federal law in the future. This issue was endlessly debated by lawyers, but a number of older expatriates felt that the word of Sheikh Mohammed could be relied upon, and that buying property in a prosperous city like Dubai made good sense.

Sheikh Mohammed had apparently been concerned that Emaar Properties' first towers at the Dubai Marina were not selling well on leasehold, and that the initial international response to his ambitious artificial Palm Island project off the Jumeirah Beach had not been good. He therefore decided to get the real estate market moving by making an announcement on foreign ownership, and at the same time decided to cut the prices of villas on Palm Island by 50%. The iconic project sold out within a week, and the rush began to bring forth new projects to satisfy a clearly unsatisfied demand for real estate in Dubai.

In March 2002, AME Info published its first of hundreds of articles on Dubai real estate, and set the scene for a lively debate that has not stopped since:

'Early indications are good. The first two towers on the Dubai Marina sold out quickly and there are not many apartments left. The nearby Emirates Hills combines self-build options for larger properties with ready constructed schemes such as the Andalucia development of large-size villas. Here many villas are now under construction and agents say that the past month has been a good one for sales. So are Emaar Properties a realistic investment option? There is no doubt that for rent-paying expatriates intending to stay more than five years in Dubai then it pays to buy a home if you can.

Simple economics show that it is better to end up owning a home than having nothing to show for years of renting.'

But this had to be balanced against the risk of exposure in such a new and unregulated property market, and the same article noted:

'The second-hand market remains an unknown for expatriates, who have not been able to own property before. But of course, property changes hands all the time between Dubai nationals, so a market does obviously exist and an active one too judging by the recent levels of real estate transactions. On the other hand, if there is a downside risk, there is also considerable upside potential. Anyone who bought an apartment in Hong Kong or Singapore in the early days will be a happy person today. For how many people have you ever met who lost money on bricks and mortar in the long run? And how many have regretted not having done so?'

A later editorial took this argument a stage further, and boldly stated:

'However, the investment case looks an open and shut job by any rational criteria. In the worst scenario, you are no worse off than if you rented a property in Dubai. And even if rentals fall, mortgage payments rise and house prices drop, you would still have the cash stored in your home that would otherwise have been paid as rent. So even if Dubai property does not prove to be the bargain it looks right now by any international standard, anyone buying on the generous mortgage terms now on offer cannot really lose. Seldom do such opportunities occur in a lifetime, and those who do not take up this option now will kick themselves hard in future years. Perhaps the England football captain David Beckham and his wife came to this view while on the Dubai beach before the World Cup football tournament. They are said to have decided to buy a $1.5m villa on the Palm Island in Dubai.'

By September 2002 when expatriates returned from their summer vacations the real estate fever had gathered pace, and another article on the website summed up the feeling of the time:

'Looking out of the window of AME Info's brand new office in the Dubai Media City, and listening to the banging of hammers below, there is quite a panorama. The new hotels next to the Royal Mirage are nearing completion, the Palm Island is sprouting out into the Gulf, and the Knowledge Village will be a low-rise across the frontage of the AME Info building. Peer from the rooftop and the six towers of the Dubai Marina apartments are half completed, and further up the piling has started on the Jumeirah Beach Residence. Several hotels and more apartments are also going up in this area.

'Cross the Sheikh Zayed highway and Emaar Properties is building a new town of thousands of villas, the Emirates Hills and Emirates Lakes, home to this correspondent. And nearby are the further phases of the Dubai Internet City (DIC) and DMC. Where on earth is all the money coming from? On the Emaar side, the answer is easy. The $3 billion initial public offering five years' ago left the company cash rich. Projects like Palm Island and DIC are Dubai government territory, and usually funded from the cash flow of the preceding project.

'There is also much reason to be cheerful about the emirate's economic future. The Dubai technology and media free zone will employ around 50,000 staff within two years, and the even more ambitious Dubai International Financial Centre is coming up quickly behind it, another $2 billion building project. Such white-collar wealth will surely be a solid foundation stone for the nascent housing market – and freehold ownership for foreigners is only a few months old – and cements Dubai's status as a regional hub. A generalised regional political breakdown seems the only credible threat, and Dubai has lived with regional instability since forever.'

But even at this early stage people fretted about oversupply and the majority of expatriates remained firmly sceptical and decided to stay out of the market. It was a decision that many would later regret as the boom developed. But without a time machine you cannot take advantage of a property boom with the benefit of hindsight. It is a matter of being bold when others are fearful, and taking what at the time appears a huge risk but later looks a very wise and even lucky move.

My wife and I considered our own position. I had seen property booms and busts before as a journalist and saw a clear opportunity in the market reform just announced by His Highness. Fortunately my wife is an ex-property developer from St Petersburg in Russia and also has considerable experience of real estate. We still looked long and hard at the market place before deciding to buy. And I was one of the one thousand people who queued up in the Emirates Towers' Godophin Ballroom that autumn for the chance to buy in The Meadows off-plan, an Emaar planned community. In fact, I gave up when asked to commit so much money on the spot against a revised floor plan, but we went back a few days later to the Emaar sales office and found that a few villas were still available.

It would be untrue to say that having bought myself this did not influence my writing. But I liked to think that having put my money on the table this also gave me an additional interest in the outcome of the Dubai real estate experiment. That is what it was in 2002 because foreigners had not been able to own property before. The doubters had a whole string of objections, each of which could easily be the subject of an article.

The New Year saw an optimistic reassessment of the market:

'Down on the ground AME Info's investigation of the marketplace showed very low availability – in short most developments are practically sold out, with only the least desirable properties available. Damac, for example, has just one two-bedroom apartment in The Waves left at the back of the property. Go over to Emaar Properties' The Greens opposite DIC and the situation is worse, no more two-beds will be released until June or July at the earliest. The second-hand market – still mainly for off-plan options – is lively but premiums paid above the original asking price are rising. There have been some cheeky ones, such as the eleven villas fronting The Montgomerie Golf Course, $682,000 up from $490,000. At least in this case you can see what you are buying. Not so at The Palm, Jumeirah where premiums of 20-40% are being paid on the selling price for off-plan options, with two years or so until completion. However, these are all healthy signs. The doom-mongers predictions of masses of unsold apartments and overstretched developers do not seem true, although it is still hard to convince some people that all these apartments and villas have actually sold, and that there is not a massive conspiracy in place.'

At a personal level I found that a number of old friends thought I had gone completely off my trolley. As if launching a dotcom venture after the US dotcom crash was not bad enough, this guy was buying property in a completely untested market with no legal rights whatsoever. I asked my old legal chum Nigel Truscott for his advice and he said, 'As a lawyer I would have to advise you not to do it!' David Price, who later bought an interest in AME Info for HSBC Middle East, looked at me as though I was bordering on insanity. He offered 'ten good reasons not to buy' and meant it. From my perspective it seemed that we would never again have a chance to buy at such a low price, and that the legal issues would be sorted out and raise the valuation. My wife just said she thought it was something we ought to do, and if we got an 80% mortgage there was not a lot of our money at risk.

That May I wrote a piece comparing property prices in London and Dubai, using the classic Martian observer as a guide:

'Imagine Martians abducted you and took you to Mars, and quite unexpectedly then asked you to choose between two pieces of real estate. Property A. is a small one-bedroom apartment on the edge of a large, old, prosperous city; cost $400,000, expected gross rental yield 5.3%. Property B. is a five-bedroom, four-bathroom villa in the centre of a new, rapidly growing, prosperous city; cost $400,000, expected gross rental yield 8.2%. It would not be a tough decision. Property B. offers a 50% higher return on capital, and the accommodation is four to five times cheaper.

'What if the property market in the location of Property A had been going up for 10 years, while Property B was located in a city with an entirely new property market yet to publish its real estate law and develop a mortgage market? Again, advantage to Property B. Clarification of legal status and availability of finance are two major factors likely to push up capital values. Plus markets rise and fall, and after 10 years Property A is ripe for a correction (i.e. a price fall). Ah, but what if the supply of Property B was huge while the supply of Property A was hamstrung by a shortage of land and planning laws?

'Well, for one thing location would still count for something as not all the property supply could physically be in the same place, so a good location for Property B would be a hedge against oversupply. Besides, what if building cost inflation had just taken off in the city of Property B and not the other one? Then in order to build the 'huge' volume of homes developers would face higher and higher costs, and therefore have to raise prices, so early buyers would still have a bargain. Moreover, inflation would eventually make development unprofitable and choke off supply, again leaving early buyers with a capital gain and a limited housing stock. Coming down to earth, Property A is located in London Docklands and Property B in Emirates Hills, Dubai.'

The sceptics were unconvinced, and this strong line of adverse comment continued while we waited for our new villa in The Meadows to be completed. It was impossible therefore not to resist having a dig at the opposition after moving into our new home in March 2004. The article began on a note of reflection:

'When my wife and I reserved our villa in The Meadows the Iraq War had not yet happened, and the geopolitics of the Middle East looked particularly wobbly. But after eight years, six independently and two together, in Dubai we were convinced that the UAE would continue to prosper whatever else happened in the region. Also, Emaar Properties had the longest track record of any developer, and we could actually see villas built by Emaar. Indeed, to make doubly sure we were living in a town house rented from Emaar at the time, and had occupied this villa in Emirates Lakes as a newly-built home. We were impressed by The Lakes management team, and nothing in our home buying experience was much different. The staff was courteous and efficient, and business times were always to suit us and not them.

'Obtaining a mortgage from Emaar's Amlak Finance, then the sole home loan company in the UAE, was also straightforward. As a former UK house buyer I was familiar with the paper chase involved and the approval process was swift. We also got pretty much what we asked for, an 80% loan over 15 years. As the handover date approached we made frequent trips to see the house under construction, and there was never anyone to stop us. Thus when it came to the final inspection we knew what to highlight, not that there was much beyond a few scratches, and the lady assistant seemed to notice rather more than us.

'We seem to have been very fortunate in our contractor. Arabtec delivered the villa exactly on time. In fact one month ahead of their original schedule, so we were able to move in just a few days after the handover date. Why pay rent when you can own? Emaar's new customer care centre was unfazed by our appearance at 8.15am on the handover day, and the keys, forms and a very useful customer handbook were all ready. This pre-emptive strike allowed the installation of curtains and blinds and kitchen appliances before we moved in, as well as the checking of air-conditioning and connection of water and electricity.

'Did anything go wrong? It was not perfect. One air-conditioning unit was not connected and three water heaters. A kitchen unit door needed changing to accommodate the dishwasher, a small design error. Several toilets, a hand basin and the washing machine (installed on the day of arrival by Emaar's Emrill subsidiary) developed minor water leaks. Were there any hidden charges? None whatsoever! Where we did immediately decide to spend more was on the garden, and to build a patio with doors into the villa.'

This also seemed like a good time to speculate on the future of the Emirates Hills district where we now lived and to contrast its advantages with older areas of Dubai:

'First, many people like a planned community with landscaped streets, an abundance of greenery and fountains, and private security. Jumeirah, by contrast, still has sand between the houses and unsightly huge dustbins strewn around the roads; and house breaks-ins are sadly more common. Secondly, the quality of construction in the Emirates Living zone is higher than in Jumeirah, where private landlords have haphazardly developed villas with little architectural input besides a brief to squeeze as much as possible onto a small site.

'Thirdly, rental prices in the Emirates Living are far below the inflated levels of Jumeirah, which reflect supply patterns of the recent past. Why pay Dhs a 200,000 a year for a five-bedroom home in Jumeirah, when new-build in The Meadows starts from Dhs115,000? Fourth, there is the convenience factor. The city of Dubai is growing in the Jebel Ali to Sheikh Zayed Road corridor, and Emirates Living is bang in the middle, while Jumeirah is more suitable for downtown Dubai. So how long will it be until rents in Emirates Living are higher than in Jumeirah? This is surely the ultimate test of a location. A reasonable guess is that as soon as the holes in the road are filled and the villas are fully completed and occupied, then Emirates Living will be the next Jumeirah, and rentals will move sharply upwards.'

This indeed proved to be the case, with rents at The Meadows tripling within three years and house prices six-fold by late 2008. But it was not all plain sailing for the Dubai property market and whereas building villas in The Meadows was a fairly simple exercise, constructing the giant Palm Jumeirah artificial island took far longer than originally anticipated. The optimism of the early days was infectious.

'We are right on schedule,' a senior Nakheel official is quoted as telling AME Info about the Palm Jumeirah. 'The villas will be ready by the end of 2005, the trunk apartments in the second quarter of 2006, and the crescent projects by the end of 2007. We are pushing the developers to get their projects ready so that this can all be done quickly. It is our credibility as a developer that is on the line and we will not risk damaging our reputation.' Inevitably this construction schedule soon slipped far behind.

At the same press conference the late Butch Kerzner, Nakheel's business partner in the Atlantis Hotel to be built at the far end of the Palm Island, announced, 'We think this is such a great project that we have decided to go ahead immediately with the second phase, and add an 800 room hotel tower bringing the total number of rooms to 2,000.' Kerzner's group is the owner of the huge Atlantis Resort in the Bahamas, and is exporting this theme park and resort hotel concept to Dubai. The Dubai project includes a 40-acre water theme park including an aquarium where guests can swim with the dolphins.

It was in this heady atmosphere that Dubai property prices began to take off and in July 2004 AME Info wrote:

'Dubai is going through a real estate boom, and prices have really picked up this summer. But at the top-end of the market real estate is now changing hands at London and Beirut prices. Consider the Golden Mile on Palm Island, where a two-bedroom apartment will cost around $750,000. Or the recent example of the Burj Dubai Residences, here a one-bed apartment that sold in phase-one six months ago for $200,000 is now $325,000 in phase two. How long will this continue? Judging from global market experience, the uptrend in property markets usually lasts longer than expected and there is an element of prices shooting beyond sustainable levels. Dubai does not seem to have reached this late stage of the property cycle just yet.

'Indeed, some agents say Dubai is halfway into a three-year property cycle. If that is true then selective buying still makes sense. But in a market that only came to life two years ago with the creation of freehold ownership, such judgments are a tough call. On the other hand, there is massive liquidity in the Dubai real estate sector, with lots of equity, and very little debt, as the mortgage finance industry is also still in its infancy.'

Looking back the agents' verdict was not far wide of the mark. Property prices hit a new peak in September 2006 with a final price spike after having been pretty stagnant for most of that year. When this comment was made the Dubai boom was just beginning, and in the subsequent 18 months prices accelerated and buying off-plan and then re-selling shortly afterwards at a profit became a highly lucrative trade for this short period. Those who knew when to stop made fortunes out of this flipping of property, and it was remarkable in the unwinding of this trade in partly-constructed property how few speculators got really burned, at least in the initial weakening of the market into 2007. Only in 2008 were a few off-plan projects cancelled and investors handed back their money.

Yet in January 2005 the Government of Dubai continued to take full advantage of the enthusiasm of investors for new real estate projects. With oil prices high and the West less popular for investments in the post-9/11 climate, Dubai was cashing in on regional liquidity and trying to soak up as much of this available cash as possible. An article from that month on AME Info summed up the mood of time:

'In recent months Dubai Crown Prince General Sheikh Mohammed bin Rashid Al Maktoum has presented three new mega-projects: the Palm Deira – bigger than the previous two palm islands, Dubai Business Bay – an extension of the Dubai Creek with a massive business free zone, and now the Dubai Waterfront next to the Palm Jebel Ali.'

'There is still room for new projects,' he told assembled dignitaries at the launch. 'Our policy is not to wait for others to think on our behalf, but to continue with our march towards prosperity and building our future.'

Not for the first time had Sheikh Mohammed's vision for Dubai left observers lost for words. AME Info commented:

'The same reaction followed the announcement of the first Palm Island project and the Internet city free zone some five years ago. Both projects are today considerable successes. Companies are queuing up for space in the Dubai Internet City and unfinished homes on the Palm Jumeirah change hands for a substantial premium. Indeed, with the benefit of hindsight, both projects could have been much bigger. This lesson appears to have been absorbed by the Dubai planners – and this is a city that does its homework and much time is spent on infrastructure development ideas. Thus development projects are now larger from the outset, albeit in phased structures that allow for the ups and downs of the business cycle.

'In many ways the model followed is Sheikh Rashid bin Saeed Al Maktoum, the creator of modern Dubai and father of Sheikh Mohammed. In the late 1970s Sheikh Rashid took advantage of the huge flow of petrodollar investments during the oil boom to build the enormous Jebel Ali port, which became the Jebel Ali Free Zone. This was a mega-project that looked incredibly ambitious in its day, and in real terms the actual investment is still bigger than any single modern Dubai mega-project. But the Jebel Ali port laid down the infrastructure that allowed Dubai to thrive as a trading centre in the 1980s and 1990s. Without Jebel Ali Dubai would not be the city it is today.'

All the same, many observers wondered where all the money pouring into Dubai real estate was coming from. In April 2005 the chief executive officer of Dubai Holdings, Salman bin Dasmal, told the Australian Business in the Gulf luncheon that according to his organisation's best estimate around $300 billion had returned to the region, out of around $1 trillion held overseas at the time of 9/11. He said that most of this money had returned to Saudi Arabia, and from there a lot had found its way into Dubai real estate, as well as regional equity markets. 'This is not a new observation, although the figure of $300 billion is new and a bit higher than most observers' estimates,' noted AME Info. This insight certainly helped to explain how projects worth $100-200 billion emerged in Dubai during the 2000s real estate boom.

The private sector also became increasingly aggressive. It was not just the government-backed Emaar Properties or directly owned Nakheel and Dubai Holdings that took the initiative. Private sector companies like Damac Properties grew from nothing into large concerns while the Dubailand theme park marked an enormous change of direction.

Dubailand is designed to entertain and amuse the 15 million tourists a year Dubai intends to attract by 2015 and will vastly add to the hospitality infrastructure of the emirate. This is to be nothing less than the leisure and entertainment hub of the Middle East. However the sheer scale of this project left AME Info asking:

'Can Dubai swallow the City of Arabia? The largest shopping mall in the world, 35 towers from 45 to 70 storeys high and a dinosaur theme park featuring 35 animatronic species. Even by Dubai standards the Galadari brothers' City of Arabia, part of Dubailand, is a challenging project. Ilyas and Mustafa Galadari, scions of the famous Dubai family, have taken on this massive development with completion slated for 2008, but what appears an impossibly ambitious scheme is actually a far more realistic business proposition on closer inspection.

'For Dubailand the Dubai Development and Investment Authority has adopted a unique public-private partnership business model – which is actually a more complex version of the traditional Dubai technique of business expansion, namely you go to the ruler and ask for a piece of land to develop. In this case the DDIA established the framework of the project first, and then the land deal was negotiated with Ilyas and Mustafa Galadari. Nobody knows how much was paid for the land, but the development model is clear enough. The next step was for the Galadari brothers to sell on most of the land plots for developing the towers to investors. The clever part is that the land is worth much more as a part of an active development project than pure desert outside Dubai. Thus the Galadaris will net sufficient funds to at least partly offset the construction cost of the giant mall which is linked to a dinosaur theme park.'

All the same, when the Galadari Brothers placed their order in Japan for several hundred life-sized dinosaurs to attract visitors to the largest shopping mall in the world, siren voices began to be heard again. Would this mark the high watermark of the Dubai real estate boom? Would the City of Arabia actually get built? Or would the Galadari brothers suffer the same fate as their father who lost his fortune in the mid-1980s property crash? The next chapter will follow the supply and demand dynamics of the Dubai real estate market which emerged from 2005 to 2007 and where the boom is going next.

7

The Dubai Real Estate
Boom Matures

From the vantage point of the Montgomerie Golf Club's terrace there is a magnificent view down over the Dubai Marina and into New Dubai. Even in the year 2000 this was just an empty patch of desert with a recently completed 1.8 kilometre artificial marina. But by 2005, where this chapter picks up the story of the Dubai real estate boom as seen from the pages of the AME Info website, more than 100 high-rise towers had started to emerge in this compact area facing the famously wide and sandy Jumeirah Beach, and also across the Sheikh Zayed highway at the Jumeirah Lake Towers.

Regular visitors to the Monty's terrace could not help but be amazed by this sight. At first it looked as though a field of mushrooms were pushing their way through the sand. Then the spindly tower cranes sprouted, and finally the towers themselves glinted against the midday sun. A similar picture might have been drawn for many Dubai mega projects, from the Palm Jumeirah to the Dubai Festival City site, or the DIFC. Everywhere the sound of pile hammers echoed against concrete and floors rose skywards at dizzying speed. Some three floors per week were added to the Burj Dubai, set to rise to around 170 storeys, and become the tallest building in the world.

However, in 2005 the ever-popular Dubai Property column on AME Info as, frequently the best-read article of the week as compiled automatically from our log-file data, correctly judged that the boom was not over yet. Opponents were a lot thinner on the ground by this point. Rising prices and flipping properties had made quite a few people rich, while the sceptics found that their rental costs were now surging, leaving them poorer both in investment terms and in their monthly outgoings compared with a mortgage. At this time Dubai share prices were also heading to giddy heights, and AME Info even suggested that a share crash would be a good thing for property prices because more cash would flow into real estate. The Chairman of Damac Properties, Hussain Sajwani, dismissed this idea from AME Info as 'completely absurd', but it proved correct nevertheless.

Referring to GCC stock markets, one AME Info article suggested:

'A very clear price spike is sticking out a mile, and anyone can see that even an economy with fantastic prospects can not maintain exponential growth in share values. Conventional valuation yardsticks, such as price-to-earnings ratios, point to considerable over-valuation. Now if GCC stock markets undergo a significant correction, there will still be huge liquidity in the region, but investors will be wary of stocks. Thus real estate is likely to be a beneficiary, and fortunately real estate prices do not look particularly high just yet.

'For example, compare the cost per square foot in Dubai with a small town in southern England. You will find UK investors presently accept a rental yield about a half of that found in Dubai, and that house prices are double. The degree of undervaluation is even greater if you try to draw a comparison with London prices, which is not so unfair given the value of tax-free expatriate salaries. So from the standpoint of international benchmarks Dubai property is not overvalued at all. Therefore, once speculators have done with GCC stock markets we can expect them to turn their attention more exclusively to real estate. The implications for prices are obvious.'

This price comparison with the UK drew some sharp reactions from local financial advisers such as Stephen Corley of Paradigm who said he wanted to 'rip out the throat' of the person writing this article. His argument was that the legislation surrounding property in the UK contrasted with the absence thus far of real estate law in Dubai, and that therefore UK real estate was an inherently safer asset class. I would not necessarily have disagreed with him on this assertion, it was just that the upside potential on Dubai real estate seemed greater as a consequence.

Presumably Mr Corley's blood pressure shot up again in the summer of 2005 when we warned:

'Tempus fugit! If you have been waiting to buy in Dubai then you should get a move on. Prices in the re-sale market have picked up again, and are going higher. By international standards Dubai property is still cheap but that may not last for much longer. Estate agents in Dubai report that the re-sale market has sparked back to life after several dormant months. Possibly the sharp increases in local rental costs are forcing potential buyers to reconsider, and this is still the best reason to take the plunge for any long term Dubai resident. If you are renting a villa in Dubai, how much rent did you pay last year? $32,000? How much will you be paying this year? $45,000? Spare a thought for one-bedroom apartment tenants in The Greens. They paid around $11,000 last year and this year $16,000 is the going rate for annual rent.

One way to fix your accommodation cost is simply to buy in Dubai. Hopefully in time your salary will move higher and your property valuation will also rise. What is the downside risk? First, interest rates may increase although long-term US interest rates are not likely to vary very much from present levels. Second, you could want to move abroad, but then you could take advantage of the high rental costs of Dubai by renting out your property. Or the market could collapse. But how much would you actually lose then? If you kept your property, rather than selling it at a cheap price, then you would not lose anything as you would just wait for the price to recover in due course. You would, of course stand to lose even more if you continue to rent – and that loss is guaranteed. In the villa example given above, with rental inflation, we are talking about a guaranteed $300,000 thrown out of the window over five years. On the one-bedroom apartment in The Greens renting will cost you about $120,000 in lost savings. Unless you are an eccentric millionaire, that is a lot of money.

'For buying a house is somewhat akin to a savings policy and rolling up your mortgage payments into an account for a rainy day. If you carry on renting you can be sure of one thing, you will have nothing after years of paying high rents except your happy memories! This is an investment nightmare, and those who are sitting on the sidelines in Dubai do seem to have started to wake up. Rental increases have been a nasty alarm clock, and this is just the start. For the UAE is a rapidly growing, booming economy and the pressure on existing accommodation is becoming acute. The pain and anguish of those who have already missed out on the first three years of freehold Dubai property will be nothing compared with the abject despair that they will suffer in the next three years or so.'

However, times were changing as the Dubai freehold revolution moved into its fourth year. As we noted on AME Info:

'Delays on delivery are not new in Dubai, but waiting times are getting longer. The Meadows 3 and 4 came in two months late just over a year ago, now slippages of more than six months are the norm. This adds to the pressure on the existing housing stock. Last year some 250,000 new residents moved into Dubai. Now even allowing for the fact that perhaps only a quarter needed upscale housing, this still amounts to more than 60,000 people in need of a home. If a new housing project is late those people still have to live somewhere. That adds to the competition for the existing housing stock and allows landlords to jack up the rental rates. Actually the market does this; landlords just pick up the cheques.'

An article in July 2005 summed up ten factors supporting the case for further price rises and the case was pretty overwhelming:

1. Rents are very high

   Ask anyone how much their rent has gone up in 2005: 10% and they are lucky, 50-65% if they are not. Against a background of stable to moderately rising house prices in 2005, rental yields have therefore taken a sharp upward movement. This attracts investors into property, while pushing those renting into buying in order to avoid future rent rises – and who says Dubai is not growing fast enough to push rents higher again in 2006?

2. Prices are low

   Compare Dubai to a prosperous UK city and you will find that house prices are around one-third per square metre. Tax-free incomes in Dubai compare more than favourably with UK post-tax income levels, and borrowing costs are similar; this huge price differential clearly marks a market opportunity, not as big as it was three years ago, but still big enough.

3. Mortgage costs are falling

   Local and international banks and financial institutions in the UAE are producing more mortgage options by the day, and the net effect is to lower the cost of borrowing. If it costs less to own a home in Dubai then this has to be good for prices.

4. New federal law

   A new federal property law is expected this autumn: this would remove a major area of uncertainty for investors and increase the pool of investors who would consider Dubai a possible investment option. More investors will be good for prices.

5. Supply short in key areas

The inventory available from Dubai estate agents is relatively small compared to the massive influx of new residents expected and still arriving (there were 250,000 in 2004). Try to find a one-bedroom flat, it is tough even now: imagine how difficult it will be this autumn.

6. Demand high in key areas

The rapid expansion of Dubai as a business and trading hub for the Middle East is bringing in more and more expatriates. There is huge pressure on the existing housing stock: hence the massive rental increases this year.

7. New supply is delayed

For all the talk of over-supply the reality on the ground is a serious shortage of accommodation. This is compounded by delays of a year or more on many high profile construction projects. It is a moot point as to what the impact of this supply will be eventually, but at the moment its absence is the more significant factor in the market place. Besides, what is being built? Is this where the most demand lies? If not, then shrewd investors can still invest wisely in the alternatives.

8. UAE economy continues to boom

Oil revenues are sky-high, economic reform is happening fast, and Abu Dhabi will be next to invest hugely in its domestic infrastructure. Dubai will be happy to supply and contract to meet this ambition next door.

9. Dubai is becoming famous

No city in the world is presently more successful at marketing itself than Dubai. Foreign investors are already active buyers of local property and may buy more. Dubai has advantages as a tax haven. These are only just being recognised.

10. There are still too many sceptics

Consider this view of market psychology: in any investment market the top can only be truly called when almost all the participants are convinced that they can not lose. This is not yet true of Dubai property. There are many sceptics; otherwise this article would simply be stating the obvious. Indeed, a few sceptics have cashed out this summer, perhaps when they are buying back into the market in a year or two's time that is the moment to be really nervous! The cycle is not at the top.

As if this catalogue of positive reasons was not enough, another article that summer turned the sceptics own scepticism back on them as an argument supporting the Dubai property market:

'The idea that a property market might crash when it has the highest rental rate growth in the world is clearly absurd. But that is what a few diehard pessimists continue to predict. Usually these people are bitter because they failed to buy earlier when prices were much cheaper, and hope that somehow their own opinion might cause panic sales and bring the market back to a price that they would be comfortable paying. Market theory of human behaviour recognises this phase of the cycle where the believers in the market's strength are still faced by a hardy bunch of disbelievers; it predicts that this shows that the market still has more room to run higher, as the disbelievers are still available buyers that just need to be convinced! It is only when all the players are in the market that you should start to worry about the possibility of a market top.'

But the local real estate market was changing and maturing even at this point in the boom. The move by investors away from speculating in off-plan sales was matched by a new interest in buying villas. As an early villa buyer this correspondent found this understandable and asked why people were beginning to prefer buying villas and not apartments:

'One reason is that villas represent better value for money in terms of space per square foot. High-rise is more expensive to build than low-rise, so you get less space for your dirham in an apartment. Thus villas are cheaper than apartments, and also come with gardens which many expatriates seem to like. Another issue is supply. On some estimates there are around 80,000 units under construction in Dubai, of which perhaps 15,000 are villas and 65,000 apartments. Clearly villas in the best locations are going to be scarcer than apartments, and that scarcity should mean higher prices.

'Then there is demand. The Dubai expatriate community has a marked preference for living in villas: hence the popularity of Jumeirah, which is the prime expatriate area and principally a district of low-rise villas. This market preference was also apparent from the early days of Dubai property launches. Emaar Properties found that it had huge demand for the few villas on its first phase of the Dubai Marina, even when the apartments were harder to sell.'

By October 2005 the Dubai real estate market showed another sign of maturity when HSBC announced that it would begin offering local mortgages, and AME Info published an article that is among the best-read articles of all-time on the website. It explained:

'Pioneer home buyers in Dubai three years' ago faced a short-list of one company when arranging a mortgage; Amlak Finance was the only place to go. Since then Tamweel has been created as a local rival, and several local UAE banks have entered the mortgage market, most recently the Abu Dhabi Commercial Bank. HSBC has been in the market for a while, but was offering finance on a very limited selection of Nakheel properties. Now this giant of international banking has rolled back the frontier a stage further with its flexible mortgages.'

New finance is good for any market, especially from a trusted global household name like HSBC. But in 2005 the first cracks emerged in the until then breathlessly optimistic outlook for Dubai business with the stock market hitting a top in June then crashing and recovering into November and then heading down again. In point of fact the world's best performing stock market in 2005 turned into its worst performing market in 2006. As we have already discussed in this chapter the redirection of stock market cash into real estate actually gave the boom another burst of life. But the market was now differentiating between property locations, types and developers and by no means every development showed uniform progress.

This article summed up the year-end position;

'The year 2005 was a tale of two markets: re-sale of completed property continued strongly with prices either holding steady at higher levels, or advancing 10% or more in the case of villas; but off-plan sales slowed considerably, and the first negative premiums emerged on certain developments, such as The Golden Mile on The Palm, Jumeirah. At the same time 2005 was also the year that hyperinflation arrived in the UAE. The Central Bank says nominal GDP growth was 20% and actual growth 8%, which means core inflation of 12%. Given UAE interest rates are around 8% that means a negative real interest rate of 4%. Negative real interest rates are generally extremely positive indicators for property markets. However, house price inflation has not been running as high as consumer price inflation, so there is no need to get too carried away.

'What we have to ask for 2006 is whether property investors will begin to feel that real estate prices have lagged too far behind general inflation, most notably rents. For it is a fact that rental yields for property investors went up in 2005 thanks to average rental increases of 38%. Meanwhile, there is an awful lot of real estate under construction in Dubai, and this is leading to fears of oversupply. But this supply will not even begin to come available until the closing months of 2006. Thus 2006 is a difficult year to judge. We have a very strong macroeconomic factor like negative real interest rates pressing up against a phenomenal building program that looks like the sword of Damocles hanging over the future of the market. So a safe overall conclusion would seem to be that 2006 will see prices holding steady for completed property, but with the possibility of some weakness towards the end of the year.'

In January 2006, the Dubai Property column asked the question whether buying was still a good idea, and concluded:

'From a pure investment point of view, it is now harder to make a case for buying Dubai property. There is a large oversupply of property of certain types – mainly middle to up-market apartments – due in 2007, and this is almost certain to lower rentals and at the very least keep nominal Dubai property prices contained at present levels. But at the end of the day, a decision to buy a property is a personal thing, and the answer on whether to buy is always a matter of considering your individual circumstances.

'For somebody intending to make Dubai their long-term home then buying is down to three factors: saving on rent; using a house as a savings policy; and the pleasure of being able to do what you want with your own home, subject only to planning constraints. The last factor is the hardest to assess objectively, as it is a subjective criteria. Some people love the idea of the Arabian Ranches, close to the desert and with an equestrian theme; others thrill to the idea of stepping from their Dubai Marina apartment onto the beach at the weekend.'

Indeed, the waning case for investment in Dubai property was underlined by a new house price index published in early 2006, from the Investment Boutique, modelled on the UK's well-respected Halifax House Price Index. It showed that 2005 was indeed a tale of two markets, with villas performing substantially better than apartments. In fact, the average price per square foot of a Dubai villa improved by 31% over the 12-month period. But the average price of apartments fell by 10% in the first half of 2005, and then rebounded back in the second half, to close pretty much exactly where it started.

However, 2006 was not a bad year for Dubai real estate as it turned out. Delays in the delivery of new projects continued to push back the date of likely oversupply, and the long-awaited Dubai Property Law was finally decreed. This meant that for the first time foreigners could register properties under their own names in the Dubai Land Department. And if the latter conjures up images of Dickensian title deeds think again, this department offers the very latest in electronic land and property title registration.

As AME Info noted:

'Previously buyers held a contract of sale from the developer which allowed transfer of ownership only through the developer, with an agreement in the contract that a full and unencumbered freehold title would be granted on the property as soon as it became available. Indeed, the biggest practical impact may be felt in the local mortgage market rather than the re-sale market. Some international banks, notably Standard Chartered Bank, have not been willing to enter the mortgage market due to the legal uncertainties surrounding ownership rights, duties and obligations. Now presumably Standard Chartered Bank and others will enter the mortgage market and begin to force down the cost of mortgages with aggressive pricing and new products.'

Indeed, by the spring of 2006:

'A brief glance through the ever-thick pages of the Gulf News property sections, and there are three of them, confirms that price levels are up in 2006. If you look at apartments in The Greens or villas in The Meadows you will find that 10% is about the going rate of house price inflation so far this year. How can this be explained? Well, we are looking at completed property, available for occupation, and not one of the many towers emerging from the ground in the Dubai Marina and Jumeirah Lake Towers district. Perhaps there is a second wave of investor interest in the Dubai market now that Gulf stock markets are turning downwards. In classic investment theory a real estate boom will typically accelerate after a stock market crash due to a shifting of funds from one asset class to another in a search for solid value. It has to be said that Dubai property is still attractively or at most fairly valued, and that does leave some room for speculators to drive prices to more exceptional levels. Yields on Dubai villas of 7.5% compare very favourably with 2-3% available in more mature markets like the UK, and are therefore attractive to investors who will drive prices higher and rental returns downwards.'

In the few months after the new Dubai Property Law was decreed on 12 March, AME Info recorded 14 new project announcements in Dubai. The developers ranged from the local stalwarts Emaar Properties and Damac Properties, through local secondary developers, to big international names from Korea and India with three projects worth $775 million. Topping the list was the Dubai-based Fortune Group's $1.1 billion commitment to building the 108 storey Burj Al Alam in the Business Bay district, with 27 floors of serviced apartments, commercial offices and the world's highest hotel. Rising 480 metres, the Burj Al Alam is designed to resemble a dazzling crystal flower.

The City of Arabia also launched its Wadi Residences, 1,600 apartments in five-storey buildings at the heart of its city-within-a-city plus the dinosaur park and the world's biggest shopping mall. Meanwhile Dubai-based Al Manal unveiled its $816 million Crown City residential project with 8,000 apartments in 52 buildings in the Dubai Investment Park. Emaar Properties released the last of its popular Alvorado villas at the Arabian Ranches around its golf club, and also reported rapid sales of its first offering within The Old Town Island at the Burj Dubai Downtown – The Tajer Residences – comprising 252 individually designed waterfront apartments.

Aside from the $1.1 billion Burj Al Alam, there were four other major project announcements at the upcoming commercial district Business Bay. Tulip announced its Peninsula Tower, Al Attar Properties launched The Skyscraper, Tameer rolled out The Regal Tower and leading Korean firm Bando Housing Corporation bought land for a $350 million mixed-use development. New Dubai also saw some major new development projects: the $323 million Taj Exotica Resort and Spa, The Grandeur Residences on The Palm Jumeirah from ETA Star, the $191 million Palm Island hotels from Zabeel Investments and TUI Hotels and Resorts, and the Iris Blue, a 29 storey residential tower in Dubai Marina from Sheth Group of India.

Had all these diverse property companies got the Dubai property market wrong? AME Info concluded:

'Perhaps if these companies were mainly international and not Dubai-based this might be a fair conclusion. But the majority are local concerns, generally run by local businessmen with a good track record, and usually self-made, not the usual candidates for throwing money away. However, one thing that is quite certain is that the Dubai Property Law has revived the launch of new development projects in Dubai. Whether this continues and for how long, only time will tell.'

Then in April 2006 the Dubai Government trumped all these announcements with The Lagoons project, an $18 billion investment. At 70 million square feet The Lagoons is the largest development project of the twenty-first century so far. It will comprise seven landscaped islands linked by bridges, with residential buildings, shopping centres, office buildings and marinas. There will also be a central business district, five star hotels, an opera house, theatre, planetarium, art gallery and museum. All the property at The Lagoons will be sold freehold to all nationalities, and half will be sold to third party developers. The balance will be developed by Sama Dubai, the realty arm of Dubai Holding, which is 100% owned by the Dubai Government.

Meanwhile, Colliers International published an 'Office Market Overview for the Gulf Region' which highlighted a doubling of Dubai office rentals since 2002, and the fact that 40% of current tenants were tentatively looking to increase their office space. The conclusion was that the office market would remain tight until mid-2007. However, Colliers also noted that the present 14 million square feet of office space in Dubai will more than double to 28.7 million square feet by the end of 2008, and that there is a substantial amount of new build office space in the pipeline to come after that, such as the Business Bay office towers and now additional space in The Lagoons.

AME Info reported:

> 'The potential for an oversupply of office accommodation in Dubai from the middle of next year is therefore clear, even if the present situation is definitely one of undersupply and not oversupply. Indeed, 'Property Weekly' has pointed to a surge in secondary sales in the Jumeirah Lake Towers office developments and a doubling of prices since 2003, underlining the current strength of the office market. Of course, The Lagoons will be a phased project, and not all built in one go. Sama Dubai will spread the development over a timeframe

dependent on demand from investors and end-users. But this project clearly supports those local observers who contend that the real estate market is heading for oversupply in key sectors, such as luxury residential apartments and shopping malls.'

This correspondent had started to feel that the game was almost up for Dubai property in mid-2006, far too early as it turned out. Prices continued to surge in 2007 and 2008. But in August 2006 the website published a final article on the boom which predicted a final price spike in September. This argued:

'In terms of rental yields Dubai property offers one of the best returns available in global property at present. Dubai rents have rocketed due to a shortage of completed property, and so the return for landlords is high. This factor alone ought to guarantee at least one more upward movement in prices before the inevitable correction – perhaps as new supply kicks in later on next year. In short, market forces should push house prices sharply higher to produce falling rental yields.'

In fact this final spike forecast proved spot on, at least for 2006, and in the autumn Standard Chartered Bank unveiled its new house price index, which showed that prices had indeed spiked in September. From this point onward AME Info began to report in a more negative fashion, bringing howls of derision from the likes of Stephen Corley who accused us of changing our tune. But as Maynard Keynes once remarked, 'When the facts change I change my opinion, what do you do Sir?'

The fact that emerged as blindingly obvious in this case was that a huge supply of property was being built in Dubai. A report from EFG Hermes precipitated a tidal wave of debate on the supply and demand issue. Dubai has a demand for 40,000-50,000 residential units per year, said this study and 69,000 units are to be delivered in 2007. But, more alarmingly, in 2008 it said some 139,000 units are due to be handed over, although delivery dates in 2008 are even more likely to slip than in 2007 as only 14% of these units will be completed by large developers, compared with 75% in 2007.

The AME Info Dubai Property column remarked:

'This study highlights a fear prevalent in the local market that while the outlook for 2007 is sound enough, it looks as though supply and demand will be getting seriously out of kilter by 2008. EFG Hermes' main scenario for Dubai is a period of stability in 2007, followed by a cumulative 25-30% fall in property values by 2010, albeit "the range of potential price decline outcomes is very wide". The major caveat is that this analysis is predicated on there not being any significant slowdown in the economy which would weaken the flow of expatriates into Dubai. So if oil prices came unstuck in the forecast period, the outlook would be very different.'

Strangely, local property developers generally took no notice, but there was a slowdown in new schemes, particularly after the rush of new projects at the Cityscape 2006 trade show in December. One thing that certainly kept the property boom alive into 2007 was the continual delays to major projects, such as the Jumeirah Beach Residence and The Palm, Jumeriah – in practice it was still hard to find completed accommodation to buy or rent in early 2007. The busting of the Dubai boom looked just a matter of time though – given the impending supply and demand imbalance – but sky high oil prices kept the local economy expanding faster than ever in 2008 and property prices accelerated upwards.

Did AME Info carry on recommending property as a buy for too long? Only time will tell. Those who bought early are sitting on an equity cushion into the downturn and Dubai has displayed resilience in overcoming overbuilding in the past. It could well be that cheap office and residential accommodation are the catalyst that attracts the next wave of financial and service industry companies to the city. Owning a property in a good location in a dynamic hub city will probably be a much better investment than many alternatives.

It is interesting to note that the completion of tall buildings almost always marks the top of the business cycle, and no city in any period has managed to avoid business cycles. For example, the Empire State Building was completed in New York in the early 1930s during the Great Depression, and remained half-empty for a decade. Indeed, it was known as the Empty State Building for much of the 1930s. Similarly, London's Post Office Tower 1966 (UK devaluation crisis), London's NatWest Tower 1974 (worst post-war stock market crash), World Trade Centre in New York 1974 (same stock market crash), Canada Tower in Canary Wharf 1990 (worst post-war UK recession), and even the Petronas Towers (1998 Asian Financial Crisis). The message is simple. Tall buildings are conceived in booms, take some time to build and are completed just as the market tops out.

In the case of Dubai the world's tallest building, the Burj Dubai, is scheduled to be completed in mid-2009. This can surely be seen as a warning sign that Dubai is in the midst of a boom that will not last forever.

8

An Apology To Dr Marc Faber

Appropriately enough I first came across AME Info star columnist Dr Marc Faber on an Internet website while searching for investment information. It was the summer of 1999 and I had just completed my first book. In the bank sat the cash from the sale of my two houses in England and it was not unreasonable to concentrate some attention on researching investment opportunities. Like any small investor at that time I could hardly fail to miss the fantastic performance of Internet stocks, although like many people I had actually missed the opportunity by the time I spotted it.

In truth, my most perceptive observation in the summer before the Millennium was that the Internet bubble would go spectacularly bust, dragging the Nasdaq and possibly the whole US stock market down with it. Strange as it may seem today, there were few analysts who shared that opinion, or would air it openly. For this reason I trawled websites and booksellers looking for a guru who might agree with my conclusion and provide some intellectual support. A revelation came when I noticed the authorised biography of Dr Marc Faber, entitled *Riding the Millennial Storm* by the Hong Kong based journalist Nury Vittachi.

This tome comprised an anthology of the recent writings of Dr Faber, or Dr Doom, as he is known in the trade. We heard how he had warned his clients to cash out before Black Monday on Wall Street, foreseen the bursting of the Japanese Bubble in 1990 and the

1998 Asian Financial Crisis. This author had benefited hugely from the availability of the lengthy and amusingly written newsletter, *The Gloom, Boom & Doom Report*, which provided an excellent prime source and treated its subject in a witty and accessible style. Dr Faber's millennial gloom more than supported my own conclusions about the future, albeit with vastly more knowledge and experience.

For any journalist with a story to pursue the next step is obviously to interview the main actor. I emailed Marc Faber's office and received an equivocal reply to my request. It was perhaps understandable that his staff were a little defensive when I turned up unannounced in his office in Hong Kong late in October, but it is hard to resist the appeal of a journalist who has come halfway around the world to see you for an interview. I was fortunate to catch Dr Faber on one of his quieter days too. He reminded me of an Oxford don surrounded by books and papers and souvenirs from Maoist China, and his dimly lit and rather smoky office belied the global status of its occupant.

We ran over his analysis. What was immediately apparent was that he had been predicting the downfall of US equities for so long now that it had to happen sooner or later. He admitted his own pessimism had considerably under-estimated the optimism of the investing public about US stocks. In fact, this failure to call the turn on US equities left him wavering a little in predicting the market collapse that I wanted to hear. I had to drag it out of him, connecting up his own logic. By the end of the interview he seemed once again convinced by his own pessimism and I did write up the interview for *Investor Relations* magazine, which was a thriving publication having grown with the late 1990s stock bubble.

Elsewhere in this book the series of events that led to the creation of AME Info are more fully described. Suffice to say that when it came to deciding who ought to be a columnist on the Middle East's first financial website, my mind turned immediately to Dr Marc Faber. I am not sure if he even recalled our meeting, but Dr Faber is always open to new ideas – despite his pessimistic disposition – and also probably spotted the benefit he could derive from a platform to promote himself in the Middle East (a major investor in global markets). Maybe the contrarian nature of our venture appealed to him. Setting up a dotcom as the sector crashed showed either that we genuinely had a good idea, and would survive to prosper in the eventual recovery, or were completely mad. Dr Faber gave us the benefit of the doubt and an article a month in exchange for promoting subscriptions to his newsletter with a click-through banner.

What we did not appreciate then was that his column would become by far the best read and most popular on the website. It proved quite an extraordinary phenomenon, and I think the best example of the leverage of Klaus' technology being applied to a first rate contributor. This technology worked wonderfully for the humblest press release, but if you applied it to articles that often came close to sheer genius then the leverage worked even better. By early 2007 an astonished general manager told me that Dr Faber's articles outperformed anybody else's by a factor of 40%, which is even more astonishing when you think his articles are long, require specialist knowledge to understand and are infrequent.

Indeed, they achieved something bordering on cult status for a column on the Internet, and on a Google search always appeared immediately after Dr Faber's own website. The quality of the articles rests on their accurate investment calls, and a consistent record. Any regular reader of investment commentaries knows that over time most advisors get it wrong almost as often as they get it right. The difference with Dr Faber is that he is significantly skewed towards being correct, and very clear and direct in his conclusions. He once modestly said that any journalist could write a positive or negative article about him by picking out his good or bad calls. However, just as Nury Vittachi could sit down in the late 1990s and pen a book that sided with the positive view, this author has scanned over more than a hundred articles for AME Info in the 2000s and reached a very similar opinion.

So what did Dr Doom get wrong in the 2000s? Not a great deal really, but actually his biggest error was a repeat of the error of pessimism he committed in the 1990s. This time it was about the length and durability of the US stock market upturn after the second Gulf war in 1993. In the 1970s Dr Faber had known Alan Greenspan as an adviser to his then employer on Wall Street and he retained a low opinion of this gentleman from that time. Yet his own warnings about US stock overvaluations dated from around the time of Alan Greenspan's famous 'irrational exuberance' statement in 1996, and were also just far too early. Hence when I met him first in 1999 he was often dismissed as a "permabear" by his detractors.

What he missed entirely was that the start of the second Gulf war in spring 2003 would be a "bottom war" marking the bottom of the US stock downturn that began in early 2000. He thought US stocks were down and would fall still further. For example, in December 2002 Dr Faber wrote on AME Info:

'I believe the present stock market rally in the US will shortly run out of steam – possibly between now and January of 2003 and thereafter, we will likely move into a trading range and eventually make new lows – maybe only in 2004 or 2005!'

He kept on calling a downturn in US stocks, admittedly catching a few corrections with some precision.

His record on the US dollar was much better, and in February 2003 he was perfectly correct in saying:

'In the course of 2002, we have repeatedly warned that US dollar weakness was only a matter of time. Since the summer of 2002, the dollar has weakened considerably and we feel that the 1995-2002 bull market has definitely come to an end and that, after a brief technical rally, more dollar weakness should be expected in 2003, as the US economy continues to disappoint.'

In the event, the nominal US stock market rally was then supported by the declining value of the US dollar, and the value of US equity investments, if denominated in non-US dollar currencies, drifted sideways. So in that sense Dr Faber's pessimism about the performance of US equities throughout the 2000s was proven correct as US stocks went nowhere in foreign currency terms. Indeed, on many occasions he elaborated this thesis, explaining how a depreciating currency can reinforce the illusion of a rising stock market despite a weakening economy, Zimbabwe being the most obvious modern example. But still, even the most ardent admirer of Dr Doom could see that his predictions on the nominal price moves in US equities proved too pessimistic in the 2000s as in the 1990s.

Except that he was completely right as regards the Nasdaq. In October 2000 his AME Info column noted:

'This Nasdaq 5000 level may very well turn out to be as much of a 'milestone' in financial history as the Nikkei 39,000 level reached in December 1989. When the Nasdaq reached in March the 5000 level, this Index consisted of about 4800 stocks with a market capitalisation in excess of US $6 trillion. Based on combined Nasdaq earnings estimates for the year 2000 of US$25 billion, these stocks had, in March 2000, collectively a P/E of about 240!

'Now, let us assume that the Nasdaq with its $6 trillion valuation can grow its earnings at a compound rate of 20% per annum for the next ten years 'without interruption.' At the end of the period, in 2010, let us also assume that the P/E of the Nasdaq will be twice its earnings growth rate (of 20% per annum). In other words the Nasdaq will sell for 40 times earnings. Since the S&P 500 sells for about 28 times earnings, the assumption of a P/E of 40 for the Nasdaq is quite realistic. Under this scenario, the Nasdaq's current $25 billion in earnings will grow to $155 billion in ten years time and with a P/E of 40, these $155 billion would have a value of $6.2 trillion.

'In short, even under this extremely and, in my opinion, totally unrealistic scenario, the Nasdaq would at best be in ten years time where it was in March of this year. Thus, I personally, would not be surprised if over the next 18 months the Nasdaq instead of showing rising earnings would actually have flat or even down earnings. Now, think what would happen to the valuation of high tech stocks if sometime over the next few years the present high tech boom is replaced by a high tech bust! In my opinion, Nasdaq earnings, which might then amount to anywhere between $25 to 40 billion would be valued with a P/E of maximum 30 to 40.

'Thus, the market capitalisation of the Nasdaq would add up to somewhere between $750 billion and $1.6 trillion, and this would correspond to a Nasdaq Index of between 800 and 1800. In other words, there is the possibility that the Nasdaq could fall from its March high of 5000 by more than 70%. I know, some readers will say that I am nuts, but the Japanese Nikkei also fell by more than 70% from peak to trough as well as most of the Asian markets after 1997. So why not the Nasdaq, which is valued far more dearly than these other markets ever were?'

With the benefit of hindsight this was a superb application of sober investment analysis to the dotcom boom folly that still held some investors fixed like rabbits in car headlights even in late 2000. As we now know, even seven years later the Nasdaq was still only worth half of its 2000 peak! This part of the US equity story in the 2000s was accurately foretold by our guru in Hong Kong. Yet, as superb as this insight was, Faber's most brilliant call of all was undoubtedly to buy gold at the start of 2001, way ahead of most other market commentators and following a 20 year bear market that had left the gold market in a mood of deep depression and despondency. This incredibly radical call first appeared in an article in February 2001 with a groundbreaking fundamental analysis of the gold market.

'Today, I should like to advocate the purchase of a group of stocks, which has over the last twenty years been the worst under-performer. This group consists of gold mining companies around the world, all of which have a combined stock market capitalisation of only $30 billion. In other words, you could buy the world's entire gold mining industry for just $30 billion. A bargain when you consider that Cisco and Microsoft alone had earlier last year a combined stock market capitalisation of more than $1 trillion, and that Amazon.com was valued at its peak at $35 billion! In addition, the market value of all the world's gold mines is tiny when compared to the world's total stock market capitalisation of around $35 trillion. Before going into my main argument for investing in gold and gold shares, let me discuss some of the gold market's fundamentals.

'Every year in the 1990s, physical gold demand has exceeded the annual supply of approximately 2500 tons – valued at present at about $35 billion – by about 300 to 500 tons. Compare this to the annual supply of bonds in the world, which amounts to about $3.5 trillion and it becomes evident how small the supply of gold is. Then consider this. In the year 2000, Indians bought about 850 tons of gold. In other words, in India, where the GDP per capita is only $300 per annum, every man, woman and child bought almost 1 gram of gold each. If gold became one day as popular as platinum or the Nasdaq is at present, and every person in the world bought just one gram of gold, it would generate an annual demand of 6000 tons, which is about 2.5 times its annual supply from mines.

'Also noteworthy is the fact that the outstanding gold short positions amount to between five and eight years of production. So if a gold market rally took place – for whatever reason – massive short covering could drive the gold price far higher than anyone currently thinks possible. Then, if we compare the price of gold to the Dow Jones Industrial Average in the US, it is clear that gold has never been as cheap as right now. In 1980, when the gold price reached more than $800 per ounce, you could have bought with one ounce of gold an entire Dow Jones, which at the time was hovering around the 800 level. Today, it would take you more than 40 ounces of gold to buy a Dow Jones. Ergo, stocks are now by historical standards high, while gold is extremely low.

'So, why is it that gold has performed so poorly when the fundamentals for buying gold seem to be rather compelling? Gold has performed poorly, especially given the above mentioned imbalance of demand over supply, because central banks in Europe have been massive sellers of their gold holdings over the last few years. Moreover, there may have been some concerted effort by the US Treasury, the Fed and a number of banks to depress the gold price through active market manipulation. It has been alleged that such manipulation of the gold market was designed to artificially depress the gold price in order to give Americans the impression that there is little inflation in the system, and also to protect some financial institutions' huge short positions. Should the gold market rally in earnest, the gigantic short positions could never be covered, given the fact that they amount to a multiple of the annual supplies.'

Probably nobody has written a better assessment of the fundamental case for investment in gold, and at the same time Dr Faber also correctly called for an emerging market stock rally based on a resurgent China that also had an important message for the commodity markets in general:

'Let me offer some thoughts. In China, increasingly, domestic manufacturers whose competitive position is improving will squeeze out foreign companies such as cellular phone manufacturers, which relied heavily on selling their products into China. Also, as more and more foreign companies start to produce in China, its domestic economy will remain robust and lead to rising property prices in the long run. In this respect, I believe that Shanghai properties are one of the most interesting investments at the present time. In India, I can see that the software industry will continue to grow. The Indian software industry will not only penetrate the domestic market but it will also gain market share from software providers in Europe and the US thanks to its cost advantages.

'India's drug industry will also grow rapidly, since it will largely ignore foreign patent rights and over time develop more and more its own drugs. In Thailand, it is obvious that in the long run the manufacturing sector has little chance against Chinese manufacturers, but as China becomes more prosperous, Thailand's tourist industry will thrive on the back of zillions of Chinese visitors. Similarly, natural resource producing sectors of countries such as Malaysia, Indonesia, Vietnam, and also Australia and New Zealand will do well as China may one day become the world's largest importer of commodities such as coffee, cocoa, copper, plywood, timber, grains, and meat.

'At the same time China will expand its political clout in Asia and as a result will also become a capital exporter to Asian countries, which are of some strategic importance such as Myanmar, Cambodia, the entire Central Asian region and Far East Russia. In fact, the Russian Far East could be for a while a major beneficiary of China's growth as it can supply China with all its resource wealth. Asian opportunities aside, I incidentally believe that the Russian stock market has over the next two years the greatest up-side potential.'

Indeed, by the middle of 2001 Dr Faber had made the critical market judgments that would be the subject of his classic investment book, *Tomorrow's Gold,* published at the end of 2002. This book correctly forecast the bull market in commodities, particularly for oil and gold, and the growth of emerging markets. Dr Faber broke the classic emerging market business cycle down into phases from zero through to six. In brief, zero is a bombed out market post-crash, phase three the peak of the boom and six the loss of all hope. In early 2003 I posed the question in another article on AME Info asking the question: 'Where is the Middle East now in terms of this business cycle sequence?'

'My estimate is that most of the real economy is in phase one ready for take-off, while the UAE, Bahrain and Qatar are already in phase two with a boom in place. At the same time the investment market is still largely stuck in phase one, with Kuwait and Saudi Arabia showing the first signs of phase two. This suggests that many of the investment markets in the region offer excellent value right now. Dr Faber says he likes to sell out in phase two of the business cycles to avoid the more uncertain phase three as the boom develops. Moreover, Dr Faber is very emphatic in believing that a 20-year bear market for commodities is now behind us. That is clearly excellent news for the Middle East and oil revenues. It suggests that the oil revenues of the past three years are the new status quo and not an aberration caused by world events.

'Indeed, Dr Faber links the present boom in commodity prices to easy money policies by the Federal Reserve and other monetary authorities around the world. This has clear implications for asset prices in the Middle East and other emerging markets. Dr Faber thinks $1000 to $1500 per square metre for apartments in prime locations in major cities is now cheap. For those buying real estate in Dubai at less than $1000 a square metre this is clearly good news. His point is that commodity price rises will kick off inflation in the value of real assets and that the US dollar will devalue not so much against other currencies as against commodities. Thus buying real assets like equities and real estate is a very good idea in the Middle East, and equities linked to oil are a particularly good buy.'

How true that all proved to be, but you needed a framework of analysis to understand what was happening in the Middle East at such a crucial juncture, and Dr Marc Faber provided it in his book. In fact, the business cycle section of this book is just as applicable today, except of course that everything has moved on through the phases. Dr Faber gave the Middle East in 1980 as a typical example of stage three of the economic cycle and this was again clearly recognisable in the mid-to-late 2000s in the region. He explains this phase as typified by: inflationary pressures and supply bottlenecks, a sudden and unexpected fall in stock prices, rising credit and leverage in the system, frequently one of the world's tallest buildings is about to be completed, a new airport is completed and another in the planning stages, stocks and real estate become topics of conversation everywhere, foreign money inflows are highest, and acquisitions boom. Surely anybody living in Dubai or Doha in 2007-8 would recognise this picture.

But the next phase Dr Faber calls "Down cycle doubts" and this has some very different characteristics. For phase four is marked by a slowing of credit growth and a deterioration of corporate profits. Excess capacity in phase four is a problem, though seen as a temporary phenomenon. Stocks may stage a recovery from the phase three sell-off with foreigners who missed out before the main buyers. But in phase four some financial stress starts to become evident and non-performing loans begin to emerge – apartments are now too expensive for locals and are mainly sold to foreigners, commercial property rents reach a peak and tourism arrival growth slows. However, in phase four economists continue to publish optimistic reports and the reversal of the uptrend is not generally appreciated.

'Is the Middle East not now moving out of the "Boom" period and into something closer to the phase four?' asked this article on AME Info, concluding: 'Such modelling can never be precise and the length of each phase is very hard to predict'. Yet that takes us on to consider the next phases of the cycle, phase five and six: "Realisation" and "Final Capitulation". These are the much harder times seen most recently in the 1998 Asian financial crisis, for example. Our Swiss-born guru describes the gloom of phase six as a mirror of the optimism of phase three. The good news is that the cycle then starts all over again. In the context of the Middle East the oil price is clearly the driving force behind the economic cycle, but the emerging market business cycle is one that has been observed in many markets under many different circumstances. Those who believe 'it is different this time' are usually the most prominent casualties in the downturn.

Perhaps this is Dr Faber's greatest contribution to unravelling the complexities of the business cycle. He provides a framework that can be readily identified and applied to different economies that nonetheless move through very similar economic cycles. It is not an exact science and in particular the length of the individual phases of the cycle can vary considerably according to different circumstances. From a business and investment planning perspective it is clearly much better to have some guide to the future than none at all, and a far cry from the opposing view that emerging markets are inherently anarchic and ought to be avoided.

No review of Dr Faber's incredibly popular column on AME Info could be complete without also looking at his assessment of the oil market in 2004 which forecast continued strength, and as with the earlier gold item gives a superb summary of the bullish long term case for oil:

'Since its last major low in 1998 at $12 (when *The Economist* published a very bearish piece about oil), crude oil prices have climbed to around $50 at present. The question, therefore, arises whether oil prices are headed for a sharp fall, as most analysts seem to think, or whether far higher prices could become reality in the years to come. Over the last two years we have repeatedly explained how rising demand for oil in Asia would likely lead to higher prices – this especially because we took the view that the oil producing countries in the world were unlikely to be in a position to increase their production meaningfully. At $50, one might, however, be tempted to think that oil prices are substantially over-bought – certainly from a near term perspective – and ready to decline again. Therefore, I have noted that numerous market participants have been shorting oil futures in the hope of a sharp fall...Still, I maintain the view that we may see sometime in the future far higher prices than anybody envisions.

'First of all, if we look at oil prices in real terms – that is oil prices adjusted for inflation – the real price is right now still about 50% lower than it was at its January 1980 peak. In fact, oil is now not much higher than it was in the early 1970s, when the last big oil bull market got underway. But it is important to understand that 1970 oil price increases were coming from a supply shock driven by OPEC cutting its production while large production excess capacities existed. The current oil bull market is a function of increased demand coming principally from Asia at a time when global oil production has practically no spare capacity. So, whereas we can say that the 1970s oil shock was event driven, today's oil price increase is structural in nature.'

Needless to say Dr Faber also correctly called the top in the US housing bubble far earlier than most commentators. In June 2005 he waded into the debate:

'I am well aware that some observers dispute the fact that there is a housing bubble in the US. These observers contend that for the nation as a whole house prices have not risen all that much and that the excesses only exist in selected markets. This is to some extent true but then these observers should also recognise the fact that one of the most common features of every investment mania or bubble is that the object of speculation is very concentrated.

'The uneven distribution of housing price gains in the US is clear. The biggest price gains occurred on the east and west coast and in particular in California, Florida and New England. US housing bulls also take comfort from the fact that since 1952, the value of household real estate holdings has never declined. Again, this may be true, although we must take into account that every year the stock of homes is increasing. Consequently it is only natural that the value of household real estate has a rising tendency. Still, whereas the value of household real estate has never declined in nominal terms, it has declined in real terms and for selected markets on numerous occasions. Following strong real price gains in 1971/72, 1979/80, 1986/87, inflation adjusted prices declined in 1971, 1974, 1981/82 and in 1990/91. Therefore, following the extended period of real price gains we had since 1997, it is more than likely that prices will decline at least in real terms at some point in the future.'

Our Swiss investment adviser also firmly grasped what a US housing downturn meant for the global economy. As far back as June 2004, when the US housing market was booming, he wrote:

'In particular, I am concerned about the US housing market. In some areas of the US, housing prices have been rising at almost 30% per annum in recent years and overall prices have doubled since 1997. The question, therefore, arises when this housing boom, which was fuelled by ultra low interest rates and allowed people to refinance their homes, will come to an end.

'This is an important question because US consumption since year 2000 was not driven by capital spending and employment gains, but purely by asset inflation in the housing market, which allowed people to take out larger and larger mortgages and spend the additional funds (well understood, 'borrowed funds') on consumer durables such as cars and consumer non-durables. Now, however, there is a problem with the housing market. If the US economy continues to strengthen, interest rates, which are negative in real terms, will have to rise considerably and this could lead – if not to a housing crash – so at least to a less buoyant market.'

Dr Doom made this prediction two years before the US housing crash that enveloped the nation from the middle of 2006. Another seminal forecast greeted the appointment of Ben Bernanke in place of Alan Greenspan at the Federal Reserve. In November 2005, Dr Faber thought:

'So, at latest by the middle of next year, I would expect the Bernanke money printing press to shift into high gear. This should lead to more consumer price inflation, a weakening US dollar and tumbling bond prices. From a longer-term perspective, I expect Mr Bernanke will be the greatest disaster that has ever hit the US bond market in the 200 years of capitalistic history. So, how should investors adjust their portfolios, in light of Mr Bernanke's nomination? I am usually asked what the best investment opportunities are. Sometimes, it might be more useful to ask what the worst investment will be. I believe that the worst long term investment will be to own a 30-year US treasury bond with the view to hold it for 30 years.

'Granted, long term treasuries could rally somewhat from here for the next few months for reasons explained above. But new interest rates lows are most unlikely. With Mr Bernanke at the Fed disaster will strike sooner or later and long-term bonds will plunge precipitously once the market realises Mr

Bernanke's propensity to print money. And if extraordinary conditions warrant it, to drop dollar bills from a helicopter onto the US in order to keep the asset inflation party going.'

In June 2007 the US bond market reversed a 17 year trend and Dr Faber's call on the market seemed remarkably astute, if a little ahead of its time. Gold and precious metals continue to be his favourite asset class for the long term, if only because monetary inflation and systemic financial weakness made a higher gold price certain in his view. In December 2005, almost five years after his original call on gold, Dr Faber turned again to this subject to comment on the link between the price of gold and the Dow Jones Index, a very important indicator of the likely future direction of the price of gold.

The article noted:

'The Dow/Gold ratio has fluctuated over time between one and almost 45. When the Dow/Gold ratio was under five, gold was expensive and equities were cheap. Conversely, when the Dow/Gold ratio was over 20, stocks were expensive and gold relatively cheap. Now, it is interesting to observe what has happened since 2000. At the peak of the stock market in March 2000 the Dow/Gold ratio stood at close to 45. In other words, it was for a 'gold money' holder very expensive to buy one Dow Jones Industrial Average since it took 45 ounces of gold to buy the Dow. Thereafter, stocks collapsed into October 2002 and, therefore, the Dow/Gold ratio also declined.

'What is, however, interesting is that despite the stock market's rebound since October 2002, the Dow/Gold ratio has continued to decline. Simply put for the holder of gold – the world's only honest currency, since it cannot be printed by some dishonest central banker – the Dow, although it increased in value in dollar terms, has continued to decline in gold terms with the result that, today, it only takes 20 ounces of gold to buy one Dow Jones Industrial Average. Simply put, since 2000, gold has risen at a much faster clip than the Dow Jones and I would expect this out-performance to continue for the next few years until 'gold currency' holders will be able to buy one Dow Jones with just one ounce of gold.'

Middle East investors love to read about gold and Dr Faber's opinions are always eagerly sought about the yellow metal. It was not often that he had much to say about the region and its equity markets. That changed in June 2006 when a crash in the Middle Eastern stock markets attracted his attention. It seemed remarkable because it had occurred at a time of increasing liquidity and near-record oil prices. His view was that the problem was not liquidity, but that the rate of growth of liquidity had been slowing down. He quoted GaveKal Research as saying:

'Bull markets are like drug addicts whose next fix/liquidity injection provides diminishing returns. To get the same effects, the fix/liquidity injections need to always get bigger...Or serious withdrawal follows.'

In other words, yes oil money had been pumping into the stock markets of the region. But as Dr Faber noted, the expansion of this cash flow was slowing down, and from the end of 2005 oil production had been declining slightly and prices had stabilised. Thus while liquidity was still strong, it was not strong enough to support an exponential growth in stock market prices. Once stock markets lost their upward momentum the same multiplier effect that had pushed them upwards moved into reverse, and they had fallen back sharply. Ergo, Middle Eastern economies had experienced a tightening of monetary conditions in 2006 almost without realising it.

Yet even our Dr Doom reckoned that the regional stock market crashes might have gone too far, and in his AME Info column he forecast a 'rebound in Arab bourses by 20-30% over the next few months, although new all-time highs are out of the question'. For the Saudi bourse his prediction was spot on, but the UAE resurgence took another year and only occurred after Faber had repeated his forecast at a seminar in Dubai and appeared to spark a local rally.

He continued be a major gold bug, arguing in October 2006:

'Despite its correction from $730 to the current level, gold is still up 12% year-to-date compared with a gain of 7% for the S&P 500. I continue to believe that over the next few years gold and silver will significantly outperform US financial assets. In fact, I am leaning increasingly towards the view that both buyers of bonds and equities could get it badly wrong. The bond buyers because inflation will continue to increase despite a weaker economy and the stock buyers because corporate profits will begin to disappoint!

'Therefore, given the over-bought condition of both the US stock and bond markets and a rather poor technical picture (the new high list is not expanding sufficiently), I would certainly not rule out a more meaningful downside correction starting soon, or even a nice little crash. In addition, the US dollar has begun to weaken significantly against the Chinese RMB, which could add to inflationary pressures. So I am far less optimistic after the recent strong US stock and bond market performance than the complacent buyers of bonds and stocks. There are many factors affecting US financial assets that could in future have a negative impact on their pricing.'

I hope Dr Doom will accept this critical review of his work in the early to mid 2000s with his customary grace and good humour. We were delighted to secure him as a contributor to AME Info from the early days, and readers who followed his predictions would be generally much better off than otherwise. If you want more from the doctor a subscription to his newsletter is recommended as a class investment.

9
Good And Bad Investment Calls

Investment advisers generally suffer from selective amnesia when it comes to their own forecast record. With AME Info FN the record of successful advice thankfully more than compensates for the few slip ups, and a long-term reader of this financial website could have retired on the back of some of the better ideas. We almost always refrained from recommending specific stocks and concentrated on asset class allocation, not wanting to become known as a share tip sheet. But times have certainly changed considerably since the website launched in October 2000, just after the dotcom bubble had burst. Then, local investors were beginning to take a look at GCC equities that had crashed so dramatically in 1999, even causing a few local suicides.

In November 2000 we took a tongue-in-cheek look at how the dotcom crash had caught out the Saudi investment giant Prince Alwaleed. He is best remembered for his rescue of Citicorp in 1991 when he bought a 10% stake for $790 million, a stake which went on to be valued at more than $8 billion in late 2000. However, nobody gets it right every time and we noted:

> 'When the Nasdaq crashed in March, His Highness saw an opportunity, while most share buyers saw a disaster. He stepped in to pick up bargains, the problem is that most of them have continued to fall further, and further. The $50

million stake in the online airline ticket concern Priceline.com was acquired when the shares were $25-50, and in September the Prince bought an option to buy another $50 million worth at $25 each. Sadly the shares are now trading at around $4. This nightmare on Wall Street has afflicted the Prince's other Tech investments. The $400 million of WorldCom stock bought in April and May is down heavily. Kodak and Xerox, the Prince's hot tips earlier in the year, have also plunged, Xerox by over 50%.'

It was a bad time for technology investors who had been on a roll in the late 1990s, and even with almost vertical share charts in early 2000 the unbridled optimism of this New Era knew no bounds. Prince Alwaleed was only one of many regional investors to get his fingers burned in this millennial meltdown. The Nasdaq also proved to be a genuine bubble as even seven years later it still traded at a substantial discount to its 2000 peak, but of course anyone who put $50 million into Amazon.com or Ebay.com after the crash would be a happy person, and hopefully Prince Alwaleed held onto those stocks. However, for most people a switch in asset class was a very good idea, away from the "tech world".

In January 2001 the general manager of Emirates Financial Services, Suresh Kumar, told AME Info that he was 'cautiously optimistic' about the outlook for UAE equities, which had fallen by 16% in the previous year. He noted that the opening of the new physical trading floors in both Dubai and Abu Dhabi was a positive step, with greater transparency of results now inevitable. Mr Kumar also pointed out that general business trends in 2000 were better than 1999, and that the company reporting season should be able to offer shareholders some good news in the form of better profits and dividends. UAE firms traditionally paid a relatively high dividend and that was another attraction for investors.

This was quite a bold statement to make in early 2001, and later in the year we made one of the few actual stock recommendations ever issued on the website and highlighted the value offered by Emaar Properties. HSBC had issued its first-ever local company report in February 2001 tipping Emaar as a buy at AED2.4 compared with its 1998 high of a split-adjusted AED16. AME Info thought it should be 'a bedrock investment for any local portfolio'.

We said:

'Emaar Properties remains easily the GCC's cheapest share and trades at a price-to-book ratio of just 0.28 compared with the UAE average of 1.75. In other words the company's total assets are worth almost four-times its stock market value, and if you could takeover Emaar and sell off its assets you would almost quadruple your money. That is not going to happen because the Dubai Government holds a controlling interest. But it does mean that UAE investors lack confidence in the management of the company and their ability to deliver future profits.

'However, the latest financial results show that investors are being foolish and undervaluing one of the region's most dynamic and fastest growing companies. It now trades on a price-to-earnings ratio of 11 and a 4.4% yield. Yet this is actually one of the best managed companies in the region. In the five years since its $272 million IPO, Emaar has generated $446 million in distributable profits. Emaar presently has eight major real estate projects under development, and has published realistic profits targets for 2003 and 2004 of $176 million and $215 million respectively. What overhangs the company's share price is the rampant speculation after its IPO which forced the shares to unrealistic levels followed by a crash. But that was over five years ago, and the management has demonstrated its ability to create a world-class real estate company since then.'

Emaar stock moved horizontally for a couple of years before regaining its old strength, and eventually powered up to AED30 before it fell back to AED11 by early 2007. Of course, there was considerable trading in and out of Emaar shares on the way up. But anyone who had just bought in 2001 and held tight would have easily enjoyed a ten to twelve fold growth in capital. That was a great tip.

Even a high leverage exposure to one of Emaar's best performing property developments during the boom would have struggled to deliver such a stunningly high return. Buy and hold can be a good strategy, but you need to be patient, and not like this author who took his own advice and bought Emaar at AED2.4, only to sell for a very similar amount two years later just before the price boomed. If you have got your fundamental analysis right then sit tight, although two years can seem like a long time, especially when a share price is under water for much of that period.

However, the early 2000s were nervous times for investors. The US stock market plunged with the tech bubble bursting and the once sky-high dotcom stocks crashed to a fraction of their peak prices. In July 2002 AME Info noted another downward plunge in global stock markets with the UK giving up five years of bull market gains and the US markets more than four years of rising prices. So at that time it was more a question of spotting the bottom than calling the top.

One pointer was discussed in an article that month: the phenomenon of a "bottom war" as generally marking the low point in financial markets. We continued:

'Examples of Bottom Wars are the Spanish-American War, Second World War and the first Gulf War. For those that do not remember, the Gulf War of 1991 brought to an end the bear market in US stocks that had first started on Black Monday in October 1987. Could this phenomenon be repeated if the US decided to attack Iraq this autumn or early next year, opening the second Gulf War?'

Yes indeed this proved to be the bottom of the down cycle. I can recall that during the week the second Gulf War started an AME Info reader approached me during a press conference armed with a series of charts, the first and only time this ever happened. These charts all pointed to a market bottom always happening right before a major conflict. That was, of course, the moment of maximum uncertainty which is exactly what capital markets dislike most.

As we now know the second Gulf War was over very quickly, but that was not known at the time, only that the US was attacking another country head on, although we now know there was to be an ongoing insurrection in Iraq that still leaves the country in chaos. We also reported on another group of local business opportunists that was organising a private equity fund to invest in Iraq. I wonder how that fund performed though I never heard of it again. Spotting market bottoms is not always that easy and the expression "trying to catch a falling knife" comes to mind.

But this was the right moment to buy Middle East equities, as an editorial noted:

'The argument for buying equities now, particularly in Saudi Arabia, the UAE, and other GCC states, is overwhelming. GCC share prices have held up well over the past year, and shown some advances, but they still sell at a large discount (except in Kuwait) to the levels reached in 1998. That is clearly now an anomaly and that anomaly must be corrected by a rally in prices above 1998 levels.'

Indeed, this proved to be the start of a massive upturn in GCC stocks that ended in a spectacular blow-off in 2005.

In general, I was very wary of getting involved with promoting investment schemes locally or having much to do with the independent financial advisers. IFAs are not all conmen, and I have a few friends who are very trustworthy IFAs. The difficulty is separating the wheat from the chaff, and I really did not have the time required to do a due diligence on everybody I met. IFAs do help some people who are hopeless with their financial affairs, but only for a fee of course, and it should never be forgotten that the fee is the reason for the assistance. On the other hand, in a long career as a financial journalist I have never actually come across a person who became rich after taking the advice of an IFA. Conversely, I have come across many examples of honest folk falling foul of investment scams.

In September 2002, I attended one meeting of unlucky investors from the UAE who collectively lost around $2 million out of a total of some $300 million that had gone astray in a particularly unfortunate case. Investors showed AME Info the beautifully produced brochures and the explicit capital guarantee and certificates from Lloyd's of London (invalid, of course). There was also a distributor network that included some well-known bankers, and a top accountancy practice as auditor. The ill-starred investors argued that the distributors and IFAs that sold the fund did not carry out due diligence, and were blinded by the high commissions on offer. Perhaps the same could also be said of the investors themselves – they saw above average returns and did not ask enough questions about how those returns would be obtained.

Maybe the real lesson is that investors in the UAE, and the Middle East, should be aware of the nature of the market that they are living in. Unregulated means, well, unregulated. Nobody should ever buy an unregulated financial services product unless in very specific circumstances. On AME Info we generally harked back to the same conclusion that readers were best advised to invest money in blue-chip regulated products supplied by the large international banks, and some of the very good local banks in the region. Of courses, the fees might be higher and the claimed returns a bit lower but your money was at least reasonably safe and a big bank could not vanish into the night.

IFAs came and went. At AME Info we were caught out by the persuasive and charming characters of Towry Law. They styled themselves as a blue-chip IFA removed from the riff-raff, and hovered on the margins of many local business groups. They agreed to write and sponsor a column on AME Info and we rushed ahead and published without getting a deal signed off. Three months later and Towry Law denied all knowledge of any agreement to pay! We took the column off the website, and perhaps should not have been so surprised at the series of scandals that later led to the closure and rapid abandonment of the UAE offices of the firm. Presumably their many local clients still had recourse to the financial institutions, usually genuine blue-chips, behind the products they had sold, but doubtless many of the hopes and claims made by Towry Law proved less than entirely accurate. To see a trusted concern behave in this way just hardened an early, healthy scepticism in our approach to the IFAs. Expatriates are like fatted lambs for the slaughter in the eyes of these gentlemen, and increasingly ladies.

In early 2003 we looked very hard at the commodities market and made the following comment:

'Everyone knows that oil and gold have been rising in price this year. But what seems to have largely gone unnoticed is that practically every type of physical commodity is showing a healthy improvement in price. Indeed, annual returns for commodities read like a bull year for equities. Nickel is up 30% on a year ago, copper and platinum are strongly up. Soft commodities like cocoa, coffee, soya beans, palm oil and wheat are up by 13-60%. The Commodities Research Bureau index, a basket of global commodity prices, is up by 30% since the end of 2001.'

We took this argument a step forward:

'If we have come out of a 20 year slump in commodity prices – and most prices hardly moved in this period – then this means at least two things. First, oil stocks and oil service company stocks, and anything associated with commodities (even the Australian dollar!) are all undervalued on fundamentals. Second, inflation is out of the bag. Increasing raw material costs are inflation at its source and will be reflected in consumer prices before long.'

I suppose living in the Middle East makes you more aware of oil and gas prices, but this article boldly concluded:

'Commodities are the new big thing for investors having proven their worth in the past year by a wide margin.'

Partly this was a case of making inflation your friend rather than your enemy and in early 2004 we predicted:

The buyers of real assets – local shares, gold, other commodities and real estate – are in for a ball. For inflation in the Gulf States is happening against a backdrop of an economic boom. Under these conditions one man's price rise will be another man's wage increase, and consumer price inflation will rapidly spread to asset price inflation. Not often is such an obviously favourable investment scenario so evident. It will, of course, come to an end in future years like all booms. But things have hardly got started yet. Some GCC stock markets look cheap, like the UAE and Bahrain. Dubai real estate is one-fifth the cost of Southern England. Gold could go a lot higher as a traditional hedge against inflation. Even oil may have another excellent year as global economies recover.'

We probably ought to have taken more interest in the growth of IPOs in 2003 and 2004 in the UAE. The early IPOs did give investors a very good instant profit. The trouble was that this news spread rather quickly. Oversubscriptions grew and grew to some astonishing figures, funded by liberal bank borrowings, and consequently applications were scaled down. Indeed, it was not long before the true IPO winners emerged as the local banks that were taking fees for handling these issues and making large profits on the short-term loans used to buy them.

However, a diligent local investor who bought each IPO and held the shares would have done very nicely up until the UAE stock bubble burst. But he or she would gradually have received fewer and fewer shares as a result of the huge oversubscriptions. One IPO issue raised almost twice the GDP of the country – something of a global record – and a marker perhaps that the good times could not last forever. AME Info was a little premature in calling the top of the UAE stock market. But in December 2004 we hazarded an opinion:

'Record IPO oversubscriptions, close to 100% annual growth, valuations near to top global capital markets; these are reasons enough to doubt that GCC stock markets can continue their upward march much longer. And, yes, oil prices have started to fall.'

Yet in true stock market tradition the bulls raged on for another six months until local optimism peaked in May 2005 at the Arabian Hotel Investment Conference and the following week the market made its first significant correction. I told the person sitting next to me at that event, 'this just has to be the top of the market'. Ever youthful PR veteran Susan Furness has probably forgotten this great insight by now, even if she was listening at the time. In fact my call was a little premature because the UAE bourse staged a final rally in the autumn, reaching a new peak in November, and went on to be the world's best performing market for 2005. Being the best performing market is always a dubious distinction though, as pride often comes before a fall, and sure enough the UAE market was the second worst global performer in 2006, after Saudi Arabia.

We had told our readers to get out early, and then stay out. We were not tempted back into the market. In December 2005, AME Info suggested:

'The Ettihad Etisalat IPO was massively oversubscribed last month, and it is a pretty good iron rule of stock market investing that when everyone thinks that buying shares is a good idea that this is the time to get out, and stay out! The Wall Street legend of 1929 of how John D. Rockefeller sold out after getting stock tips from his boot-boy comes to mind. Also, Saudi stocks are up by more than 70% this year, after a similar stellar performance last year. This has stretched valuations past anything approaching reasonable, and the old adage still applies: what goes up must come down!'

And we were not that far out in January 2006 in saying:

'The prudent investor should be asking themselves: What is the upside risk? And what is the downside risk today in the UAE bourse? Cashing out while you are ahead assures success, while staying invested while the market runs ahead carries the risk of being caught in the downturn. When might that happen? Some sages say after the financial results and dividend declarations this spring, but irrational exuberance by foreign investors could bring that day of reckoning forward.'

To be fair the Bahrain office of Japanese broking giant Nomura had sounded the alarm first in the summer of 2005 with a report entitled 'The Great Arabian Bubble'. This report pointed to a discrepancy between the real economy and the financial instruments that are supposed to reflect it in the GCC stock markets in general, and in the UAE and Saudi Arabia in particular. This analysis traced the recent development of Saudi stocks and super-imposed the Nasdaq market during the dotcom years of the late 1990s and early 2000. Not only was the Saudi market's rise similar in shape to the Nasdaq, but also stock price rises in Saudi Arabia were actually significantly higher than those of the dotcom years!

Our record for investment calls on UK property was far less successful. Perhaps we were just too far away from the market. In April 2004 we thought we had spotted the end of the trend arguing:

'Many expatriates in the Middle East and wealthy Arabs have a fortune invested in UK property. Yet we all know that UK property has long run on a boom to slump cycle that extends over about 10 years. Each time the market booms many commentators come forward – usually those with a vested interest in the market – to offer the bold theory that the cycle is over this time, there is nothing to worry about, and there is nothing as safe as houses. Absolute rubbish! There has never been a housing boom in the UK which has not been followed by a bust. There never has been and there never will be. All we can be really certain of is that the credulity of investors and short-memories are a feature of the human condition.

'Just go back to the early 1990s. London was awash with negative equity, that is to say fools who bought at the top of the market in the late 1980s and then found themselves with homes worth less than they paid for them. Or go back to the early 1980s which saw a less famous squeeze on house prices. Or go further back to the crash of 1974, which was arguably the worst post-war financial crisis in the UK. So where are we now? UK house prices have been rising since March 1993. Now would it not be unusual for an 11-year upturn to be followed by a downturn lasting some years? Unless the capitalist business cycle has vanished it has to happen, and the higher things go the harder they fall.'

Like some of our other poor investment calls this one was proven right in due course, but the downturn did not come until the summer of 2007. We could perhaps have been a bit more vague. Several top City analysts have predicted falls in UK house prices of 33-44% by the end of the decade, and by 2007 this looked far more likely than earlier in the 2000s, even if the roll-out events was a little different:

> 'Interest rates are poised to rise around the world to deal with mounting inflation, and this will put up the cost of mortgage borrowing and throw a spanner in the works of the UK property boom. Confidence will be shattered and prices that bear no relation to the salaries of ordinary people will fall substantially. But most people will feel that having made so much money on UK property that they might as well hang on in case there is some more to be made. Sadly this will prove an expensive error.'

That was wrong in 2004 but by the middle of 2007 many British homeowners were feeling the pinch from rising mortgages and the world's most overvalued housing market looked very vulnerable. It crashed in 2008.

We also started to take a more cautious stance on recommending investments overseas, reporting on the view of George Soros that the slowing US housing market would be the factor that finally tripped the economy into recession, albeit not until late 2007. Soros maintained that the impact of higher energy prices on the US economy had been cancelled out almost entirely by the impact of rising US house prices to date, although inflation was up and economic growth had slowed in many economies. Again this warning proved a little premature and global financial markets rallied strongly into 2007 before tanking later in the year as Soros forecast.

On the other hand, we got it right on gold, mainly I have to acknowledge because of the publication of an excellent book called

Tomorrow's Gold by our eminent columnist Dr Marc Faber. It is astonishing to note that this seminal work was published in December 2002. Gold prices have moved from $300 to above $1,000 since then. I must admit it that personally it took me almost a year to really get the message and accept what Dr Faber had nailed down very early.

It still looked a bold call even at the start of 2004 when I wrote:

'With gold at $412 an ounce the venerable Financial Times' Lex column last week dismissed the outlook for the yellow metal as fraught with risk and liable to a sudden large contraction in price. The argument in a nutshell is that global financial markets are now back on track, have put three bear years behind them and that gold's recent strength is just some sort of a flash in the pan aberration. Let me beg to differ. I don't see how anyone can argue that the sudden and ongoing devaluation of the world's largest currency, the US dollar, is just a minor event that will correct itself given a little time. It seems to me that the complete collapse of the US dollar is an accident waiting to happen that will have dire consequences for investors.'

Once converted to the logic of being a gold bug by Dr Faber, AME Info has been very consistent in backing gold as an investment class ever since. Our articles are often prominently featured on the leading gold research websites as an expert source from the Middle East. With the creation of the Dubai Multi Commodities Centre and the Dubai Gold and Commodities Exchange locally we did often have something different to say as the gold price moved inexorably upwards.

The best year for gold before 2007 was 2006, and we took the following line at the start of that year:

'The inflation outlook in the US also gives huge cause for concern. Why would anyone hold an asset with negative real interest rates? (i.e. a US dollar deposit account?) The danger is that the so-far orderly exit from the US dollar becomes a stampede to get out of all dollar-denominated assets. That would mean a crash on Wall Street and an implosion of the bond market; 10-year US treasuries yield around 4% at the moment, how can that be an attractive investment with inflation rising? Now if Wall Street goes into correction-mode there are very few places to hide. Even the very high Middle East stock markets will not be immune from this tidal wave sweeping through the global financial community, and if US interest rates shot up to defend the US dollar then all countries with dollar-linked currencies would suffer.'

With the benefit of hindsight this analysis was correct in predicting higher gold prices in 2006 and a lower US dollar, but the strength of US equities, aside from a big May wobble, was unexpected. We concluded:

'Gold has not shared in the same powerful rally that has driven other metal and commodity prices skywards. Indeed, relative to the price of oil, gold languishes at a 25-year low, and is dirt cheap. Forget arguments about inflation and US debt levels, a simple catch-up is taking place that should send gold to $650-700 an ounce this year and possibly higher. To profit buy bullion, large mining shares, or smaller gold exploration companies if you feel adventurous.'

We also kept the faith after gold peaked at $725 an ounce in May 2006, arguing:

'The bull market in gold is not dead, it is just resting. Economic realities are very much on the side of the yellow metal, and the fundamentals needed to push precious metals to much higher prices are all in place. Indeed, it is hard to see which other asset class can deliver out-performance in such an environment. Thus Arabian investors who use the quieter summer months to stock up on large cap gold stocks, exchange traded funds, gold mutual funds, gold exploration juniors and even gold bullion and coins are unlikely to find themselves out-of-pocket this autumn, when investors in other asset classes may be in deep water.'

Once again this was too pessimistic. There was a danger growing that we would be guilty of calling a bear market downturn so often that one day we just had to be right. However, you do not usually lose money in financial markets by being too pessimistic, you lose by being too optimistic, and I saw many Middle East investors in the early 2000s believing their own infallibility only to find that they too could make mistakes, and big ones. Warren Buffett says that rules one and two of investing are not to ever lose money, and AME Info's asset allocation recommendations kept absolutely to that rule. Where we did stick our neck out was in an early buy recommendation for Dubai property, as discussed in another chapter of this book. Otherwise we certainly missed a few opportunities for big profits on investments but we did not fall into any of the major black holes.

For 2007, AME Info saw a stormy year in financial markets with precious metals again looking the most solid investment choice. But we pointed out: 'However, precious metals would likely also tumble in a global capital market sell-off, along with oil and other commodity prices.' The investment idea was to wait until the silver market bottomed in a big sell-off and then to fill your boots with silver, or silver-related assets. We noted the 45% gain in silver prices through 2006, higher than the gold price increase, and said this out-performance would likely be seen again as the supply of physical silver is far smaller than gold, and more susceptible to an inflow of speculative money.

The article continued:

'Silver behaves much like gold in times of financial crisis and is often spoken of in the same breath under the portmanteau of precious metals. But the best reason for gold bugs to diversify into silver is something called the gold-to-silver price ratio. Now the long-term historical average gold-to-silver price ratio is 16. But this relationship does sometimes get rather out of kilter. Like today when gold is at $610 an ounce and silver hovers around $12 an ounce. And not at $38 as its long-term gold-to-silver price average would suggest. This has happened because silver presently has no perceived monetary role, while the moment a financial crisis is at hand people look for quasi-currencies and silver is a longstanding currency of last resort from ancient times. What that means is that in historical terms silver is cheap in relation to gold. Even more importantly it means that in a financial crisis silver is likely to close this gap and then move in line with gold. In short, silver will outperform gold.'

This annual forecast article drew considerable attention and remained in the best-read charts on the website for many weeks. But by June the expected stock market correction had failed to arrive, despite a slump in US GDP growth to 0.6% in the first quarter, seemingly bang in line with George Soros' forecast of more than a year earlier. As a commentator you always look a little stupid with an early call. But there was a sense of déjà vu looking back at the calling of the UAE market top about six months too early. In fact, the sub-prime crisis hit on 9 August 2007 and the US stock market has not looked really healthy since then despite a rally in November. Again, AME info readers might have accused us of being a little too early, but could be thankful for the warning of what is to happen next.

10
Business Trips And Holidays

It might be considered strange to offer a chapter on holidays and business trips in a book about a dotcom enterprise, investment advice and the development of Dubai, but I would humbly suggest this is where many entrepreneurs and journalists go wrong. They focus entirely on their work in hand, forgetting to relax and recoup depleted energies, and thus when good health is most important in a busy season they fall sick. Not very clever if you have no back-up and the whole business is a shaky edifice dependent on very few people.

I always insisted on taking my full crop of holidays and building in a program of a few business trips a year, whatever the other pressures might have been. I am not sure if it really saved my health or that it did much good for sales, but I certainly enjoyed myself more than otherwise, and work should not be entirely about profit. If you are married then spending some quality time with your partner is also an excellent idea and creates a deposit in the emotional bank account to draw upon in leaner times. Singles just need a rest to work most efficiently.

Business trips can be a pleasure or a pain for the average executive, and as an entrepreneur I always felt that they had a double function of producing potential commercial gain while allowing for some rest and relaxation or just a change of scene. I was also fortunate as editor-in-chief of AME Info that the opportunities for travel generally exceeded the time available, so I could pick and choose. Usually I tried to arrange business travel at points in the year when activity was at a low-ebb in Dubai and the weather at its hottest, and it can get very hot indeed in Dubai with the mercury occasionally topping 50°C in July.

My first business trip with AME Info broke this primary rule about avoiding excessive heat and I ended up in Muscat with Lars for a series of sales meetings. It was incredibly hot and very humid too. Beads of sweat rolled off our backs as we stood waiting for the Ministry of Information's car. The Oman Government kindly offers these cars to visiting journalists – partly I suppose to monitor who and what they see on their visit, partly out of an old world courtesy which is rather charming.

Lars appeared impressed that an editor-in-chief of an as yet unpublished website could command such attention. The Omani people are friendly, kind and cautious and the nearest we got to an interrogation was a cup of tea with an undersecretary at the ministry who talked about his time as an undergraduate at Exeter University. We also met the head of the local stock market, who maintained that his French was better then his English so I changed language. Just for once it was not only the Danish with a bilingual capability – Lars and Klaus used to converse at high speed in Danish from time to time – though my range of expression in French is far more limited.

The business aspect of the trip fell a little flat since, despite their exquisite turbans, smiles and genuine curiosity, we could not excite one iota of commercial interest in our product in the Omani people. Our hosts listened intently, agreed on the wonder of the Internet and in later years launched their own business website which languished in obscurity, but everyone in Oman seemed to have a government job and no reason nor inclination to do more than converse intelligently and pass the time of day. Many visitors find this delightful, but it was not too constructive for AME Info.

In the summer of 2001 I faced a dilemma. The news service was by then in full flow, and wholly reliant on me tapping out the news briefs into my computer early each morning. So how could I possibly take August off? The situation was even more acute in that by this time I was happily in a relationship with my future wife Svetlana and most anxious to show her England for the first time, and also eager to visit her home in the splendid city of St Petersburg in Russia.

I decided to take the first half of August as a proper holiday, with a visit to the small German town of Landau in Germany to see old friends for my birthday, and then a trip to St Petersburg. After Russia I updated the news from London over the Internet for the second half of the month, rising early enough to upload the content and still leave plenty of time to spend the rest of the day doing something rather more fun. We were fortunate in that we were able to borrow a very nice flat in the Barbican in central London from two friends who very kindly arranged for a computer to be set up. In fact, the porter downstairs was an avid computer buff and assembled a rather awesome looking machine from various parts. It was a bit slow but this Frankenstein's monster proved sufficient to the task, although the time difference with the Middle East made the news a tad late for Dubai. I reasoned that at the height of summer few people would notice and certainly not the sponsors who would be on vacation too.

Over the years we also managed to fit some extremely pleasant skiing holidays in Switzerland into our busy schedule. Indeed, my fortunes were pretty low in 2001 when we first took to the slopes in Wengen, my wife's first attempt at downhill skiing. The hotel and general environment of the Jungfrau region also proved a big success with its chocolate box scenery and efficient lift system. We had a Jacuzzi in the room and for a week passed the time in a way that might be expected of a successful dotcom entrepreneur.

In fact, we returned to the same region a year later for our honeymoon, choosing the nearby village of Grindelwald, famous as the place where James Bond takes his bride for their honeymoon in the film *On Her Majesty's Secret Service*. In that film Mrs Bond is sadly shot dead by the agents of Smersh on the way back from the honeymoon. We thankfully suffered no such fate. I was more concerned about my declining bank balance at this point, and I recall I thought about my bank account as I took a lift up the slopes.

The honeymoon was a wedding present from my ever-generous mother, and the wedding itself had not been an elaborate affair. We stayed in the penthouse suite of the Bellevedere Hotel, and despite the rather poor weather enjoyed ourselves immensely. These ski hotels know how to feed sporty types and the six-course dinner is de rigueur. We also found the *Frühstück* of Swiss bread and cheese highly satisfying, but then if you are skiing and on honeymoon how could life be anything else?

Almost defying my meagre budgetary resources the summer of 2002 still stretched to three long distance trips. First, the relationship between AME Info and Lufthansa had blossomed into a full-blown barter deal and so we had a large number of air tickets available which we could happily take in business class. In point of fact this relationship followed a previous paid for trip to Berlin in the summer of 2000 to see my old friend Wolfram Bielenstein. He is the former deputy head of East German radio news and had gone to work for the British construction company Balfour Beatty after the Berlin Wall fell and his radio station was closed down.

Wolfram is an Anglophile and writes very well in English and German as well as Russian. We had been friends since a business trip in 1993 when I was writing about construction in Berlin, and it seemed only natural that he should become the German correspondent of AME Info and establish our first overseas bureau in Berlin. We laughed about the "Berlin bureau", which amounted to a computer on the desk in the corner of Wolfram's bedroom. As the visiting editor-in-chief I got to sleep on the couch in the living room, and his wife Gisela served a first class breakfast.

Wolfram really worked hard for AME Info, sending out letters to German companies that we hoped would sponsor the website and requesting interviews. Thus the arrival of the editor-in-chief in Berlin was a moment of anxious anticipation for local business, and Wolfram wangled us both an invitation to the important annual Ghorfa summit of Arab business run by a well connected gentleman of Iraqi extraction who seemed happy to have us publicise this event. Wolfram had solicited interviews, always in writing as German protocol dictates, and lined up some interesting meetings.

It was always fascinating to get a different point of view on the Arab world, and even better to have an excuse to visit leafy, green Berlin in June. Wandering the streets, taking a glass of Riesling on the *Unter den Linden* looking up towards the now restored Brandenburg Gate and watching the world go by. This was pure heaven. Wolfram was always good company, and I hope he found some of our business connections useful for Balfour Beatty because we never really pulled anything off for AME Info.

Even the small *German Business Review* column always languished at the bottom of our readership charts and only the Lufthansa sponsorship kept it alive. Thankfully that was for three years and I got back for another visit to Berlin two years later, managing to fit in a three-day hotel review of the brand new Ritz-Carlton as well as a few more days on Wolfram's couch. Sadly that really did prove to be the end of the road, and with much reluctance and a few more glasses of fine German beer Wolfram and I had to do the honourable thing and close the Berlin bureau. It was a great friendship and travel experience but not a successful business venture.

Another very pleasant business trip came in August 2002 when Emirates Airline invited AME Info to cover its inaugural flight from

Dubai to Perth in Western Australia. It is roughly a 12-hour flight overnight and with the time change we arrived in darkness, and went straight into a meeting with the premier of Western Australia. I have seldom felt more worse for wear at a press conference, but managed to put a couple of tricky questions to the Premier to show AME Info was still awake. Then we headed off to the Burswood Hotel, a large hotel with a famous casino. In Muslim countries casinos are banned so naturally most of the Arabic journalists went straight to bed and did not decide to stay up the whole night gambling and chatting to the ladies of the establishment. It certainly did not appeal to me, and my finances were in no condition to accept gambling losses at that time.

Over the next couple of days we toured Perth and Freemantle, checked out the Perth Mint, cruised down the river to a vineyard, and attended the official party for the Emirates launch which featured the Irish Riverdance dancing troupe. I then needed to get back to Dubai to pick up my wife for our flight back to Europe, so I abandoned the pack of journalists who headed off down the Margaret River for a couple of days, and had a day to kill alone waiting for the plane. The Western Australia tourism office offered a few suggestions and it was an easy choice: lunch with the owner of the Sandalford Winery at the estate restaurant.

He was feeling particularly pro-Dubai having just won a lucrative contract to supply the Jumeirah hotel chain with his fine wines, and Western Australia does boast an impressively high percentage of the best wines from the continent. We sampled rather a lot of them over a hearty lunch designed mainly around its capacity to absorb alcohol rather than any other epicurean standard. There was also a very fine port. The owner asked which bottle I preferred and I had to admit that I liked them all, so he generously gave me a bottle of each. 'Look's like you had a good time,' my wife said suspiciously on my return. 'Emirates is a good client,' I replied, which was true up to a point.

A couple of days later we flew Lufthansa to Frankfurt and then onto St Petersburg, the beautiful city of my wife's birth. I had late in life taken the only advice I remember from my Oxford philosophy tutor Mike Innwood to heart. He had said, 'Only marry a woman from a city that you would like to visit!' St Petersburg is an amazing place and in 2002 was still rather shabby and rundown from the collapse of the Soviet Union. For us it was also a cheap place to visit, especially as we stayed with my mother-in-law in her flat on a rather faceless estate some way from the centre. The apartment was built under Stalin and very solid with high ceilings and large rooms. My mother-in-law is also a first-rate cook and her takes on Russian specialties like caviar pancakes and real Russian salad were delicious.

Great though the cooking was, the real star was of course the city itself: the palaces of the Hermitage and Peterhof with their superb collections of pictures and artefacts from the great age of aristocracy, the wide boulevards of this masterpiece of neo-classical architecture, and the exquisite ballet theatres and shopping arcades. My wife once worked in the Harrods of St Petersburg, which has since been privatised, and shares handed out to all the former staff. We went off to try to locate her shares from a satellite office, only to be told that in order to prove her identity an almost impossible series of documents was necessary. Privatisation might be new but the Russian bureaucracy could still be a nightmare. On the same holiday we also wasted a considerable amount of time validating her internal passport in order that she could leave the country with me, which at one point looked in some doubt.

In London we holed up at the Grosvenor House hotel on a special media room rate arranged by a PR friend in Dubai with whom the hotel had a distant relationship. This hotel is a great base for walking around London and seeing the sites and that is exactly what we did, taking in the London Eye, Royal Academy and seeing the musical *Chicago*. Then we took the train down to Salisbury, and paid almost as much to stay in a dusty room over a pub with a very uncomfortable and ancient four-poster bed. Visitors to England should be warned about these beds whose allure is greatly exaggerated. We saw my family, caught up with a few old friends and were soon on the plane back to Dubai.

At the end of 2002 we were longing for a foreign adventure again, and as my wife had never been to Asia before we thought of Thailand, where I had spent three weeks on my world tour in 1999. It was a shame but the seaside resort of Phuket was booked solid over Christmas and New Year, so we opted for Pattaya instead. I found a bargain deal on the Marriott website and it was an impressive modern colonial-style hotel built around a tropical garden. Pattaya itself proved to be a complete dump, with the sort of Asian nightlife that might better suit a single man, rather than a married one.

To cap it all, on the first night we wandered into a local restaurant and managed to get a dreadful stomach bug. We only recovered in time to see a rather tacky elephant show before returning to Bangkok in the Marriott's rather pricey Mercedes limousine. Here we checked into another Marriott of similar style on the riverbank with a boat service into the city. We toured the Grand Palace and the Jim Thompson House, a traditional Thai house assembled by the American entrepreneur who developed the local silk trade and mysteriously vanished while out on a walk in Malaysia. My wife very much liked his silk and we bought quite a collection of Jim Thompson items. Svetlana later remarked that she has met a woman who said that the only good thing about Bangkok was Jim Thompson. I could only beg to differ. Thailand has a special style and atmosphere, though clearly not everybody likes it.

The spring of 2003 was a quiet time in Dubai with the likelihood of the Gulf War in Iraq to remove Saddam Hussein beginning to unnerve visitors. Hotels were having more trouble attracting visitors and this reached something of a crisis point in the week that the coalition actually invaded Iraq. That was the week that the 674 room Grand Hyatt Hotel, the biggest in Dubai, was due to open. I interviewed the unfortunate general manager who gamely argued that things could only get better from this point, and I suggested we review his Presidential Suite to help his publicity.

He was clearly in a desperate situation and delighted with the idea. Our own business performance was none too special at the time either, so we were happy to sample the delights of the Suite. It would be my guess that many five bedroom villas in Dubai have a smaller floor area, which must be in excess of 3,000 square feet. It is also designed to impress with gold taps, two Jacuzzis, a dining room for twelve, two seating areas, two offices with Internet and printing facilities, and endless marble flooring. This was not the place to meet your expense account auditors. The finishing touches were nice too, guests have their own butler, a huge fruit basket, fresh flowers everywhere, a massive box of chocolates and another of dates, a bottle of chilled champagne on arrival, and not a mini-bar but definitely a maxi-bar with full-sized bottles. Really the champagne and a few dates were enough.

We chose to try the Manhattan Grill as the restaurant most likely to appeal to a company president staying in the appropriate suite. As my wife commented, 'You could have been in New York, except that the service was better'. The food was certainly up to Big Apple standards with plump, fresh steaks, fine vegetables and a delicious choice of deserts. The wine list was also extensive without being exorbitant, though if you wanted to indulge your expense account this was a great place to do so.

The summer of 2003 came around pretty soon, thousands of words flowed from my computer into the website and the hot weather returned with a vengeance making an escape essential. This summer proved a little less propitious than 2002 for travel plans. I managed a very brief trip to the UK during June, on which I spent a couple of days in London in the tiniest hotel room imaginable off

Marble Arch. I had a memorable country pub lunch with that fine stock analyst Leslie Kent, a city lunch with financial PR guru Jonathan Gillen and a Browns Café lunch with Nick Rufford from *The Sunday Times* who I had not seen since his escape from Afghanistan in early 2002. Then I squeezed in a short weekend in Salisbury. It was a bit exhausting but nice to catch up with my old London colleagues and family.

For the main summer vacation we rented a house belonging to a German politics professor in Landau, which is not far from the French border and Strasbourg. This was again arranged by my old friend Jorg Saalbach who has been living in Landau since we worked together at the European Commission as trainees back in 1983-4, and I have enjoyed many happy breaks in this beautiful wine region over the years. Svetlana had liked our few days in Landau in 2001 so much that she suggested we try a longer stay.

It was just unfortunate that the summer of 2003 was one of the hottest on record in Europe. We arrived from the Middle East and immediately noticed something was wrong: the temperature had not changed. Without our accustomed air conditioning this was almost intolerable. In Landau we had to rise early and go for a walk before breakfast to catch the cool air, sleep during the day and then go out again at night with our friends. This was not quite as we would have planned it.

After a week we flew to the UK and Heathrow airport reminded me of a scene from a film about a prisoner of war camp in the Far East. Bodies were strewn around the floor and people looked seriously hot and hopeless. The air conditioning broke down on our train to Salisbury and we also had an hour to wait while changing trains on a boiling platform in the sun. Luckily we had chosen our accommodation well in Salisbury – a Landmark Trust property called the "Wardrobe" in the Close. This comprised a light and airy attic apartment with a great view over the cathedral. It caught every waft of fresh air and seemed particularly well insulated. Besides, the temperature had eased off a little! We returned to London for another hectic rush around the capital from the Grosvenor House, and then finished our month away back in our rented house in Landau which was much cooler by the end of August.

We went skiing again in Switzerland in February 2004, and Swiss Deluxe Hotels kindly arranged a special rate at the Carlton Hotel in St Moritz, rumoured to have been originally built just before the first world war as a summer home for the Czar, though never occupied, with only the Romanov restaurant as a clue to this unproven heritage. The sun shone all week and we had perfect snow, which was great after our previous disappointments with the weather on skiing holidays. We also really liked the hotel and the panoramic view from our junior suite, as well as the engaging head waiter Eugenio who had been working there for twenty-five years.

That summer was spent in the UK, at first in a tiny town house in Salisbury, then in Brighton in an old friend's apartment and finally we took a week in a cottage in the Lake District. It was wonderful to have so much fresh air after the air-conditioned indoor life of Dubai in the summer, and marvellous to still have so many friends and family to visit for reunions. There was so much hospitality with great food and wine that we needed to get back to Dubai to recover from our holiday.

In March 2005 I returned to Hong Kong for the first time since my trip around the world in 1999, with the Hong Kong Trade and Development Council as my host. The schedule was kept light and I travelled with a rather racy young journalist whose approach to stories soon got him into trouble in Dubai. He had been working in Hong Kong before moving to Dubai and disappeared with his old buddies for a good deal of the trip.

For my own part I also enjoyed catching up with my old friend from HSBC and had another chance to visit the fabulous China Club at the top of what used to be the Bank of China building. Here the elite of Asia gather for the finest local cuisine and to compete with each other to down the most expensive bottles of French wine. Obviously you need to come with a member of the club, and preferably one with a corporate expense account to entertain visiting journalists.

There was also ample reason to celebrate as HSBC Private Equity Middle East had just bought a substantial stake in AME Info, so we were in effect very distant business partners, perhaps third cousins twice removed. I was reminded of the previous China Club dinner in late 1999 during which we discussed the concept of a financial website at some length. Now the omens for the future looked propitious, and a promise was made to celebrate with a bottle of vintage champagne when the business was eventually sold. Two years later I returned, champagne in hand.

Hong Kong is a stimulating and vibrant business city with a can-do culture with a penchant for speculation. We mulled over what was hot in the investment world, and my friend agreed with me about gold, except that he had heard that silver offered an even better return. That was a brilliant tip for the next couple of years. Hong Kong is also a place that likes to champion the latest in technology and at the brand new science and technology park we learned about the possibilities of paper-thin computer displays, which must be the future of the Internet.

The most densely populated city on the planet has a notable slight aroma of raw sewage from the drain covers, which is not as bad as it sounds, and one of the world's great harbour views back towards the skyscrapers across the water. I had a quick look around the newly completed Financial Center, the tallest building in Asia, and noted that the Asian Financial Crisis seemed to have finally past in Hong Kong, although property prices were still not as high as in 1998. As mentioned this was only a fleeting visit, and after a few quick official interviews and a second pleasant night out on the town, we were on the plane back to Dubai with an upgrade to business class from Cathay Pacific – always a nice end to a trip. The HKTDC bought a $25,000 AME Info sponsorship, which made it profitable too.

Indeed, 2005 was a vintage year for business and leisure travel. I had made it back to Berlin again to see Wolfram for the last time and then in August we headed off to England once more. Saudi Arabia's legendary investor Prince Alwaleed had just acquired The Savoy Hotel in London, and this proved a handy introduction for a hotel review. The Savoy is right next to the Covent Garden theatre district and where I attended many a press conference as a young hack in the 1980s.

We dined with my old school friends Ray and Paula Bell in the splendid Rules Restaurant, the oldest restaurant in London, met up with some of my former journalistic colleagues in El Vinos and saw a play. Then we picked up a hire car from Victoria station and drove down to Salisbury and out into the wilds of the Wiltshire countryside to stay in a cottage at the bottom of Sir Frank Lampl's garden, not far from where Madonna lives. This part of the country is untouched by development and has a timeless quality. The society photographer Sir Cecil Beaton wrote about it in his famous diaries and reading them gave the place an even greater aura of mystery and romance.

It was also delightful to stay with Sir Frank and his very hospitable artist-wife Wendy, although my wife is allergic to dogs and was not so fond of their friendly old canine Eddie who followed us around everywhere. The six cats and bantam hens were more welcome, and the glorious garden. Sir Frank loves to entertain in style and appeared to have an inexhaustible supply of Cristal champagne and fine wines, while Wendy's cooking was the perfect compliment, particularly a fine saddle of lamb cooked over a barbecue. You would hardly have thought Sir Frank was approaching 80 but then he is an exceptional man and Wendy is much younger. We talked business, politics and travel, and being the historian of Sir Frank's company Bovis he likes to say I know more than he does about its history, which is obviously not true but it does leave us plenty in common that few others can share.

My mother and stepfather Alan also kept us well supplied with good food and wine as they did on all our summer vacations – venison sausages are a local specialty and grilled salmon. Alan is remarkably fit and active for a man in his mid-eighties, and he was full of good conversation on anything from art to national politics. Each summer we would have a family party with my sister, brother and their families, usually in their gardens or conservatories. It was always a pleasant gathering.

In August 2005 we took our first vacation in Yorkshire, and rented a modern stone terraced house on an estate in Leyburn, a small town in the Yorkshire Dales with a spectacular walk called the shawl on the side of a broad valley. The marketplace has some top-notch pub restaurants and we especially liked The Sandpiper's slow cooked beef. One night we met up with Ken Hanson and Professor Steve Toms, two old friends from Oxford, for a reunion in a nearby town. We also revelled in the scenery and bought a book of local walks for the Dales and the North Yorkshire Moors. It was so nice that we decided to come back the following year and did indeed make it back, meeting Ken and Steve in The Abbey Inn at the ruined Byland Abbey. Unfortunately the unpredictable British weather was not as good in 2006.

We finished up our 2005 summer holiday in St Petersburg, again staying with my mother-in-law and eating her fine cooking. This included a day visit to Pushkin to see the Catherine Palace where the Czar was imprisoned after the revolution. The rooms had been recreated just as they would have been in Czarist times and it was possible to imagine how it must have felt to be held under house arrest by revolutionaries in your own palace. On another day we took a suburban train to find the Menshikov Palace, once the home of Peter the Great's leading minister. It was fairly derelict and under reconstruction, and on a rather smaller scale than the palaces of later years. We bought mushrooms from a street seller who looked the worse for vodka and could see that not everything had changed since the revolution. In fact, St Petersburg is regaining its former glory, and we noted many improvements since our previous visit. The whole place seemed less threatening, with a definite buzz in the air and even a little optimism. We thought Mr Putin must be doing a good job, and so did most of the Russians we met.

Between Christmas 2005 and the New Year we took a ten-day holiday in Singapore and Kuala Lumpur, and decided not to go skiing in February. This came about mainly because my wife's employer decided to give staff time off between Christmas and the New Year instead of paying for an expensive party. We pondered where to go and having never visited Singapore or Kuala Lumpur before this seemed an interesting option to see some more of Asia. Moreover, my contacts in the hotel and travel sector meant that we could research a few hotel reviews at the same time and sample the famous Asian hospitality standards.

The Fullerton Hotel in Singapore gave us a smart room overlooking the river and financial district, and there was even a kind of cat-flap to collect shoes for cleaning. In the Shangri-La we experienced the luxurious Valley Wing where they accommodate visiting presidents and found the service outstanding, particularly the lobby which offers non-stop complimentary champagne. I would swear some guests never left the lobby! Of course you had to if you wanted to go shopping along the Orchard Road – one of the principal attractions of Singapore. Actually, once the Orchard Road has been sampled there is not a lot else to occupy visitors' time. Valerie Tan from Emirates Airline had kindly supplied me with a list of activities, such as taking a cable car to Sentosa Island and the night safari at the local zoo but, aside from a museum of culture and gin slings in the colonial Raffles Hotel, the attractions mainly revolved around food and shopping.

Kuala Lumpur was worse if anything. More shopping – admittedly my wife found a shoe heaven under the Petronas twin towers – and every variety of Asian food. The Ritz-Carlton where we stayed is linked to a shopping mall for top international brands and has a large complex of restaurants in the basement area. It is not a food court but really a collection of more than a dozen individual restaurants, and we saw in the New Year with a champagne celebration. The National Museum was laughable with a few mouldy old photographs of the colonial Brits, and only the Butterfly Park came close to providing a novel visitor experience. How different from the cities of Europe where culture and history surround you from morning to night. But Asia certainly has civilisation, and shoes.

11

Lunch Again With David Price

In May 2004 I took stock of my position within AME Info. The most acute deficiency from my own perspective was the absence of actual equity ownership. It had been almost a year since a final percentage of the total equity of the company was settled upon after a negotiation with Klaus. This took the percentage of web traffic generated by my section FN, and the percentage of revenue contribution, and split the difference. It seemed a little arbitrary but these formulas are seldom exact. I felt that after four years working with Lars and Klaus, and always with the understanding that an equity interest would be forthcoming, it was about time that it finally appeared in the form of a real share certificate. Also, summer loomed again and getting things sorted before the onset of the hot and indolent summer months was always a good idea.

For some reason it occurred to me that I ought to see David Price of HSBC Private Equity Middle East and update him on what had happened to AME Info. It was now some five years since he had dismissed my financial news website idea as a mere concept paper and we were certainly a considerable distance from such a dream. So I sent him an email explaining that AME Info was the fastest growing media company in Dubai with the best growth prospects, and information about our recent web traffic figures. He immediately took me up on the invitation and we met in the Wafi Mall's Italian restaurant.

Things had also moved on a lot for David Price who, with his partner David Knights, had sold his own private equity business to HSBC, and presumably done quite well financially in the process. It also meant that he now had the backing of the world's second largest bank and I could see that there was considerable value in having the HSBC name on the list of shareholders. Just their involvement would raise the value of shares in AME Info.

So I asked David Price whether he would consider buying out our existing national shareholder from Abu Dhabi, while at the same time insisting that the position with regard to my own shareholding be finally wrapped up. Over a second bottle of San Pellegrino water, for it was a hot day and this was a dry restaurant, he patiently went over the various options. I said I had heard that in some private equity deals the original shareholders got a higher stake if they achieved a particular, pre-agreed profit target, and wondered if HSBC could offer that as it would obviously help to sell the idea to Lars and Klaus?

David is one of nature's merchant bankers. He liked that sort of proposal and thought he could work something out. But the whole deal would rest on the successful conclusion of a due diligence procedure on AME Info by international firms of chartered accountants and lawyers. Private equity firms are accountable to their own shareholders and to proceed without due diligence would be due negligence.

I calmly acknowledged this process as clearly essential, though granted my previous experience of our muddled and often opaque accounting practices it did sound some alarm bells. We ended the lunch discussing holidays in Australia. David is from Perth, although UK educated with a polished public school accent, and in the heat of the Gulf the cool of the Australian summer was a pleasant thought.

Lars and Klaus eagerly took up the proposal, as they did practically any interesting business idea, and were happy to meet

David Price again. At this meeting the matter of my shareholding was raised and quickly agreed while the conversation turned to more interesting issues like the potential value of AME Info. In fact, it was not long before our national partner appeared from Abu Dhabi one bright morning at the DMC headquarters to sign-off the transfer of his shares. I never found out how Klaus and Lars had avoided the dilution of their own stakes in this process but it appeared that some other outstanding business was being concluded. This was no concern – the bigger picture view resulted in me being a small minority shareholder in AME Info FZ LLC.

However, striking the final deal with HSBC Private Equity proved to be a lot more difficult. As discussed in a previous chapter, it emerged that the accounting firm to which our accounts had been contracted out had not been issuing invoices for six months. Only in a dynamic and rapidly growing small company could this sort of thing happen. For there was clearly enough cash flowing through the bank account for Lars and Klaus not to notice that a black hole was appearing in the accounting system. But it was bad news for the 2004 revenues and profits, and David Price later remarked that this 'lost the guys a lot of money'.

Klaus had recruited a rather over qualified, and as we later found out pregnant, accountant called Jeannette Vinke to sort out this mess while at the same time concluding the due diligence with KPMG for whom she had previously worked. She had actually also been engaged on an earlier deal with David Price although he seemed not to remember. Once again for AME Info the right person came along, but this time Klaus went to a top recruitment agency and paid a very good rate for the job. We could not afford to economise on our accounting function, and had learned from an expensive mistake.

Jeannette ended up with a far bigger job than the part-time accountancy role she had been employed to undertake. Unravelling the work of our former accountants, or rather the lack of it, meant invoicing or re-invoicing clients who were not unnaturally surprised by such late invoices. Thankfully the reputation and standing of AME Info was so high that most paid up. Following this it was just a question of building an accounting system from scratch and at the same time getting a due diligence signed off. This was no small task, as many of our business arrangements were honest in intent but very awkward to fit into a normal spreadsheet, such as our ticketing agreement with Lufthansa.

Gradually these unexciting but actually important issues were taken care of and the long list of queries to be addressed before due diligence would pass got shorter. The main problem was that HSBC Private Equity could not make our national partner an offer for his shareholding until it had an audited profit figure. This was not an unreasonable view from any investor, and a legal necessity for one reporting back to shareholders.

At the same time Lars and Klaus spent a lot of time with David Price explaining how the business worked and its structure, and he became more intrigued the more he learned. I was not involved with these discussions and felt my best option was to trust the parties concerned and not muddle what was already a confusing enough situation. I had plenty to keep me occupied in any case – primarily revenue generating work with my sponsors. My instinct was that David would know the best structure for AME Info, and that this would be a part of a reorganisation that would follow from HSBC's involvement and enhance the value of AME Info as a company.

Of course both the long due diligence, reconstruction of the accounts and a new structure of the company took both time and our money in legal and accountancy fees. This naturally did not produce a dirham in additional income. Yet we realised that if AME Info was ever going to be sold then due diligence would be required for this also, and so all this work now would ensure far less effort when that time came. In addition, we knew that we would need somebody astute and experienced to negotiate on our behalf. And who would be better than David Price? Many a small company is taken to the cleaners in a takeover, but David did not strike me as the sort of guy that would be easily tricked and having the world's second largest bank as a shareholder is a bit intimidating for any potential buyer.

Therefore I kept encouraging Klaus, and as by far the largest shareholder the negotiations fell mainly on his shoulders throughout this wearying process. Yet once this was started the momentum towards a successful conclusion mounted week-by-week. It was not until March 2005 that we assembled again in the DMC administration offices to sign the documentation bringing HSBC Middle East Private Equity on board as a significant shareholder and saying 'goodbye' to our national partner who left a happy man. As ever he was very obliging in going along with our plans, but this is not too surprising because at that stage he was the only person who had made a decent sum out of AME Info. It is true that he had been very patient waiting for our success and had been a good friend to Klaus, but otherwise, frankly, he had done nothing except sign some cheques and guarantee our bank facility (which he had actually withdrawn after 9/11). Such is the life for UAE nationals who sponsor successful companies. He also did not want his name known or publicised, so he remains an anonymous beneficiary.

Now, I have to admit that the structure of the company that emerged on his departure was not quite what I had expected. My common shares in AME Info FZ-LLC became "B" shares in a newly constructed AME Info Holdings company formed in the British Virgin Islands. These shares carried no dividends but I received a 50% share of the FN division's profit, assuming there was one, as per my original agreement with Lars and Klaus.

I suppose this was to ensure that I continued to work solely on a commission basis and hence under the maximum incentive. At least it was explicitly stated that these shares would rank equally with the "A" shares in value in the event of a sale of the company and also that I could participate in the management bonus shares which, if we hit our targets, would take a portion of HSBC's stock and distribute it to us. I asked Klaus for an agreement that these bonus shares would be distributed equally and he assented in an email, so that brought me up to decent stake, close to what I had originally asked for back in 2000.

Private equity firms are notorious for forcing the pace of a business to ramp up sales to ensure that they can get the best price on an exit. HSBC was no different, but behaved in a gentlemanly and decent manner throughout, and both David Price and his partner appeared genuinely interested in this small media business with such high growth prospects. They interfered as little as possible in the day-to-day running but sat on a newly constituted board which set strategy and approved major appointments and expenditures. This ensured that the good governance practices to emerge following the due diligence process continued and also identified certain weaknesses in the business.

For a start the new board noted a lack of adequate back-up staff, and an absence of Arabic speakers, which might be perceived as a weakness in the Middle East. There was also a lot of work to be completed behind the scenes to ensure that the technical side of the website was documented and did not just rely on Klaus knowing what needed to be done. We wondered a little at the cost implications of these changes. HSBC never really needed to worry about our overspending – under-spend was more likely and this was how the accounts had got into such a state in the recent past.

Cost-effective solutions to the under-staffing problem gradually emerged. For example, our video producer Lisa had a boyfriend, Jim, who was already on our group sponsorship and offered to do some writing. Klaus suggested the news. At first I resisted this proposal but agreed to train him up because he seemed very committed to AME Info and did not want much pay, being something of a man of private means. He took some time to get the hang of the job but turned out to be excellent at it, with a legal background that proved handy for spotting potential libels.

It also made a big difference to my own workload, which was becoming onerous. By this time I was writing seven news columns a day, five days a week, keeping the features going and writing half of them, and pursuing the FN sponsors that were my only source of income. Truly, after four and a half years this could not really run as a one-man show for any longer. But Jim only did three days a week, so that made it a one-and-a-half man show. However, as a quid pro quo for this extravagant hire I agreed to add another five news columns. It was still a hard slog but at least I was now a shareholder and manager instead of a commission-only sales man and unpaid news and features writer. My wife said she could never have waited that long for things to come right and I do wonder, if I had known how long it would take at the beginning, would I have waited so patiently myself?

The first indication that a trade sale of AME Info might be possible, that is sale to an existing media group, actually came even before HSBC Private Equity had signed up as a shareholder. The original regular networking evening concept, where I first met Klaus and Lars, had morphed over time into an AME Info networking evening which gathered in the club house of the Dubai International Marine Club on the last Tuesday of each month.

One night in January 2005 the gentlemen from Emap plc turned up in the shape of the very tall managing director of the *Middle East Economic Digest*, the long-running weekly contract and business magazine, Richard Baker, and his boss Simon Middleboe. It is a small world. Simon was the guy who made me redundant from *Construction News* back in 1996 after the then Emap takeover of that publication, and that led directly to my move to the Middle East.

It really was quite a coincidence that nine years later history might be about to repeat itself, albeit with hopefully a more positive personal outcome this time. Simon was equally taken aback by my presence, and said he had absolutely no idea that I was involved. We chatted amicably over a glass of wine and caught up on old times. I had been to his first wedding but he was now on his second wife and had five children. It was just as well I had not attacked him at the time of my redundancy and had instead rushed off to the bank to deposit my cheque.

Of course, this is jumping the gun. It was clear from my conversation with Simon and his with Klaus that Emap had been watching AME Info with more than a little interest and would be interested in buying us if we could prove that things were as good as we claimed. Klaus hinted that a major bank might be about to take a stake, and Simon thought that could be very helpful in persuading Emap to buy. Richard Baker told me that he had asked his staff at MEED who they rated the most irritating presence in the local market and AME Info was always the response. I presume this referred to our instant publication of news and comment, always ahead of our paper rivals and not to my writing style. But companies like Emap are the elephants of the media world and move slowly and carefully. To be more accurate Emap is the second largest media group in the UK, so a mother elephant is the appropriate metaphor. Such elephants have big ears for listening and are directed by committees of mahouts who take a lot of convincing.

However, this was a major step forward. We had never had a serious approach by a buyer before. Klaus told David Price who reckoned it was very premature, and thinking back he might have been concerned that his own equity deal could be jeopardised by a quick offer, although equally he probably knew the score with elephants whose slow progress through the commercial jungle is notorious. AME Info would be just another acquisition in the many thousands in the history of Emap, and they had a standard approach. It was likely not much had changed in the nine years since they bought *Construction News* and fired me. Elephants are also not very sentimental beasts and often trample smaller animals underfoot without realising it.

Time also does not mean a lot to corporate elephants. Not a great deal happened for the rest of the year until Klaus and Lars decided to make a business trip to London to try to open negotiations with Emap as part of a planned sale process to find a strategic buyer for the business. In fact so quiet had things got that they kept this a secret from me and went under the cover of negotiations with CNN International about advertising. I wondered if they were trying to sell the business to CNN, but I suppose they did not want to get my hopes up about Emap and have to spend time explaining everything to me if nothing was going to happen.

However, in the first few days of January it became clear that negotiations for a sale were about to begin in earnest. This thrilled me considerably because I could see that the time and money involved in undertaking a due diligence process to buy a business would not be undertaken lightly. All the parties want it to succeed. Moreover, I was confident that with David Price on board (literally on the board) we already had our accounts and corporate governance in exactly the kind of shape that would impress Emap. He had been working hard from the moment HSBC Private Equity took its stake in AME Info to achieve that end.

David Price ambitiously hoped to wrap up the negotiations within three months. Elephants do not move at that kind of speed though, and the negotiator they appointed certainly did not. Probably as a matter of policy he liked to go slow to keep the price low. Both David and Klaus seemed to be walking in treacle as Emap returned again and again with another long list of impossible questions and enquiries about business minutia. Klaus in particular seemed on an emotional rollercoaster, saying one week that it was looking like the deal was off, and then that it was back on again. Klaus is a very cool-headed businessman indeed, so that was saying something, yet I can see that parting with an enterprise of almost ten years was a wrench even for a high price. Lars and I were on the sidelines, and really only called upon for background information, moral support and an interview at the very final stages.

There was one personal setback in this process. David Price worked very quickly to knock the final 2006 accounts into shape for the auditors. He discovered that $78,000 had been wrongly paid to me as commission, and had to ask for it back over a breakfast at the Lime Tree Café in Jumeirah. So beware of breakfast meetings with investment bankers, they may prove expensive. With the benefit of hindsight I can see that there was no alternative but to recall the money that was booked and paid in 2006, but not yet executed. There was a hopeful indication that this carry over would come back to me if a sale of the business emerged, but it is still quite a raw deal for any salesman to repay commission already honestly earned, and for me personally 2006 was the first year of what had looked like a substantial income from AME Info, and even that turned out to be illusory.

Did I get the money back? Well, this was an example of smoke and mirrors accounting, and arguably I recovered part of it but certainly not the full sum. David Price's difficult brief was to get the wrongly paid commission back from me and he achieved that. Of course, the most persuasive argument for repayment was that we all had to look at the bigger picture. This was true. The millions to be made in a sale did constitute a force majeure, but having to repay $78,000 was still quite a bitter pill to swallow with the future deal for the sale not yet done, and not guaranteed. It just goes to show that entrepreneurs do not win every battle and investment bankers are hard edged for a reason.

At the same time, Lars, Klaus and I faced a difficult challenge with the sales order flow in 2006. In the first days of January we got sad news that the Ruler of Dubai, His Highness Sheikh Maktoum bin Rashid Al Maktoum had passed away suddenly. The 40 days of official mourning that followed virtually brought commercial life to a standstill with the annual Dubai Shopping Festival cancelled altogether. This came at a time when we had committed ourselves to a highly ambitious sales target designed to maximise the final sale price. It was an awful start to the year and put Lars in particular under enormous pressure to deliver the figures. My own annual sponsorship renewals stalled badly and I waited with baited breath to see if they would follow later. Thankfully most of them did come right, but it was an anxious time.

Of course we would not have been interested in selling the business if we had not thought that the boom in Dubai was finally slowing down after a remarkable run, and that rising costs would put pressure on local profits. It was not even a matter of discussion between us. Interestingly all four shareholders had reached exactly the same conclusion about the marketplace and the agreement was so clear that we barely mentioned it. To us it seemed that the boom had gone on for an unnaturally long time, and that the real estate sector in particular looked due for a correction if not a crash like the one we had just witnessed in the local stock market. Fortunately the Emap camp saw the stock market as somehow removed from the rest of the economy and it was true that the oil price remained at a record high. We reckoned the oil price was too high to last but were hardly about to argue this point with them. Elephants stick to a set course once engaged and seldom deviate, crushing anything in their path.

The negotiations continued to ramble on and on with endless requests for more data, and I think there was a worry that this almost looked like a stalling tactic. There also seemed to be a definite personality clash between David Price and the Emap negotiator, a relationship which became pretty heated at times. Klaus would worryingly tell me that in all seriousness he wondered if it would be possible to reach a deal. In early June I went on a business trip to London to sample the delights of Etihad Airways' diamond and pearl class premium services, and also for a welcome relief from this tension. It would have been nice to be able to tell my old friends what was going on but I had to keep things pretty vague. I could see we were very close to a deal but that was not the same as having a deal signed off.

Nonetheless, I managed to sign up what turned out to be my last client as a shareholder and manager of AME Info, Orange Business Services, after an interview in the London Marriott off Grosvenor Square. Primarily I had arranged this meeting to justify my trip to Lars, who quite fairly felt a little envious of my escape at that juncture in time. In truth, it was a thoroughly pleasant trip including a five star hotel review, a few lunches with old friends and a visit to my parents in Salisbury. But while I was away the elephant had stirred and realised that matters were drifting out of control.

The onset of summer and the imminent departure of Klaus and David for their holidays seemed to draw the process to a conclusion. On 4 July Klaus, Lars and I finally visited the offices of our lawyers to sign the sale documents. The irony of American Independence Day also being our own independence day was not lost on us. It was not quite that simple, of course. However, David Price had negotiated a very tight 12-month earn-out deal and 100% sale as suited all the parties. He had done as promised and delivered a clean sale with a higher valuation for the company than we could have possibly achieved on our own.

Immediate payment is never on the cards in this sort of deal, but the HSBC involvement had achieved the best possible terms. An initial sum of $24 million went into an escrow account with actual payment phased over 18 months as the warranty periods cleared, and there was a further amount to be earned if we hit our sales targets for 2006. The bank actually chose to take its profit immediately, but left a guarantee in place which amounted to the same thing. After all if you are the world's second largest bank your credit is pretty good.

However, it was at that point that the three of us finally became dotcom millionaires, albeit without the cash in our hands as it remained in the bank on deposit for a while longer. The chances of the warranties being broken were very, very remote with our continued involvement in running the business. Klaus and Lars thought we should leave a celebration until we had completed the earn-out phase of the deal, and by that point we were all rather exhausted and beyond partying. But I had kept August as a month off and that was an occasion for a lot of private celebrations and another of our excellent summer vacations. Should I have stayed on working that summer because of the six-month earn-out deal? As it was I saw potential clients in Europe, and August is a particularly poor month for business in Dubai. And at least I returned refreshed and did not collapse in mid-September like my business partners.

The return to work after the summer holiday of 2006 felt strange. The business no longer belonged to us, and yet the earn-out stage meant that we had every incentive to boost sales until the end of December. I had a meeting in September with the new owners to clarify my position. Somewhat speciously it was claimed that my FN agreement with the company was already terminated, which was simply not the case, and given the intensity of the due diligence it was hard not to conclude that this was a try on. This was not an auspicious beginning to the autumn, but Emap relented with a letter advising me that I did still have an agreement. Well yes, in fact it was a signed legal document produced at considerable cost at the time of the HSBC Private Equity deal, so of course I did.

After that Emap kept their distance while we slogged away trying to complete our ambitious sales target. This did have an air of mission impossible as far as the sponsorship sales were concerned. The second half of the year was always a much more difficult time to close what were usually calendar year deals. In addition, Ramadan fell at the end of September so that effectively blocked a crucial selling month. By the time Ramadan came to an end December was fast approaching, and most clients would be thinking about 2007. Besides, only the portion of the sponsorship falling in

2006 actually counted towards the sales target, and the months of 2006 were fast receding.

However, it was a question of turning over every contact in the file. I also had two new real estate giants from Abu Dhabi to finally pull, Aldar Properties and Sorouh Real Estate. A couple of rather hot and sweaty trips to the UAE capital and I did manage to wrap these up. I emailed dozens and dozens of potential and unlikely customers. Of these only one actually signed up for a sponsorship. Standard Chartered Bank agreed a small weekly newsletter deal. There was fulsome praise from Emap, although apart from one lead for Arab Bank, which came to nothing, promised help from their quarter was in short supply.

This also proved an autumn when foreign travel was off the agenda and given the constant pressure to try to achieve the sales target, however implausible, there was not much time for any fun. The positioning of Ramadan in the season compressed the conference and exhibition schedule, which was consequently particularly exhausting. Perhaps too the Dubai economic boom was now running a little out-of-control. The Dubai International Conference Centre had grown and grown and walking across a trade show could mean a one-kilometre trek. PR and marketing staff were also frequently ill informed or unsure about their jobs, and this made getting things done rather frustrating.

The Cityscape real estate exhibition was typical of the almost surreal atmosphere of Dubai in late 2006. No less than $140 billion worth of real estate projects were launched that week, an amazing increase on the already remarkable total of $23 billion the year before. There were office towers shaped like flickering flames, a 40 storey revolving tower using untried technology presented as the first project of a new developer, an iPod shaped residency called the iPad, and a $40 billion entertainment and residential zone from Abu Dhabi, bigger than anything previously launched in the UAE.

You just knew that not all of this could possibly be built, not just because of the expense but also the sheer impossibility of mobilising that amount of building materials and contracts during a construction boom. When it actually pops, and no real estate boom can last forever, that is 24% of local GDP in crisis, and clearly many fingers are going to get burnt and the local banks too. But construction booms can run and run, particularly with oil prices sky high and heading higher. It continued ever upwards with oil hitting a new all-time high of $147 in early 2008.

Team morale flagged across the board at AME Info. Klaus came to Dubai less and less and Lars was absent from the office more often. The sales team was constantly harangued and I was not surprised that our leading salesman quit at the close of the year for pastures new. Emap's approach was initially hands off, and it is hard to be critical not knowing what their true agenda was for the future. But the idea of there being some common ground between a small entrepreneurial start-up company and a FTSE 100 UK company maybe expected too much.

For while it was true that we shared a similar European cultural background, Emap's view of the future was necessarily also different to our own, otherwise we would not have sold and they would not have bought us. They projected upward trend lines of growing sales into the medium term. We felt the business was maturing, with costs rising and needed a strategic owner to take it forward to the next stage. These opportunities do not come along that often, and grabbing them is essential to business success. If it later transpires that a few months or years more might have secured a better price then so what, you still have cash in the bank and time saved for leisure or the next opportunity, and as David Price once said: 'Better to regret an early sale than not having a sale.'

It was therefore quite a relief when we got to the close of December, although none of us was delighted with our performance, which fell short of the required target to get our full bonus payment.

On the other hand, one explanation for the sales shortfall was that our business had peaked in the summer and thus the business sale well timed. But forward sales for 2007 were up 100% on the year earlier, thanks to our efforts, which tended to argue the reverse. Only time would tell.

Klaus stood down as CEO on 1 January and this proved to be the start of the inevitable unwinding of the previous management. Lars also announced his plans to spend a great deal of time playing golf while remaining on hand for Emap's guidance. In the middle of the month I went to see the Emap management, which wanted to wrap up my FN agreement with the necessary three months of notice. There was a sting-in-the tail in that Emap's cost structure for 2007 would have immediately impacted on my own earnings through the FN profit agreement. In fact the most alarming projection was for a $55,000 loss, albeit including a part payment of the managing director's salary, which could be dumped on FN.

This was a pretty grounding experience. I also needed to consider the impact of the protective covenants in my original agreement that would prevent me working for anyone in a competing business for a year after the termination of my work with AME Info. Freelance work for Emap was the best option then, or a longer range project like a book which could be undertaken while under such restrictions and published afterwards. In practice both proved possible. But the more immediate outlook for 2007 was a sabbatical year with a series of holidays, particularly during the searing heat of the Dubai summer. It had after all been a long time coming and the last couple of years of the dotcom experience were very trying.

12

Epilogue: The Future Of Dubai

Since I first landed in Dubai in 1996 the local GDP has more than quadrupled. This makes Dubai arguably the fastest growing city in the world, and certainly puts it right up alongside Shanghai and Las Vegas. I have seen two booms in that period, the second one now in progress being bigger than the first. It has really been the work of one man, His Highness Sheikh Mohammed bin Rashid Al Maktoum, whose appointment as Crown Prince of Dubai back in 1995 was highly significant. It should be remembered that his father Sheikh Rashid also pursued a vision driven by huge investments that looked over-ambitious in the 1970s, but later turned into cash cows. In fact you can look right back to the granting of free trade concessions to Iranian merchants in 1901 to get them into Dubai as a shrewd business move by Sheikh Maktoum bin Hasher Al Maktoum. These business sheikhs have been ruling Dubai for more than 170 years, giving business the benefit of remarkably consistent and stable policies.

In an interview Sheikh Mohammed once explained that when his brother appointed him Crown Prince he had said that there was an easy approach to his new job or a hard one, and that he had chosen the more difficult path. It is his personal dynamism and day-to-day business savvy, as well as a clear vision of the future that has pushed Dubai forward at such a remarkable speed. He is the prince of the city state that is Dubai, and today the Ruler of Dubai as well as the Prime Minister and Deputy Ruler of the UAE since the death of his brother Sheikh Maktoum bin Rashid Al Maktoum in January 2006. Therefore, if anybody wants to know what is likely to happen to Dubai in the future they should pay considerable attention to the words of Sheikh Mohammed.

In February 2007 His Highness presented his vision for Dubai in 2015 to an assembly of senior officials, academics and business persons. His clear and stated objective by 2015 is to raise the GDP of Dubai from $37 billion to $108 billion. This sounds impressive, but in terms of annual growth this figure actually requires a slightly slower rate of growth than that achieved since the year 2000 plan: 11%, down from 13%. Indeed, reflecting back to the targets set in 2000, His Highness noted: 'In five years we realised economic achievements beyond those which were planned for a ten year period.' He also pointed to a reduction in the contribution of oil to the economy to around 5% and this is still falling.

The expansion of Dubai's GDP to the $108 billion envisaged appears entirely realistic in the context of the ongoing development of three key sectors: the free zones including the international financial centre, airports and ports, tourism and retail, and real estate. It is no more or less than a continuation of the remarkable record of high economic growth that this author has been writing about since arriving in 1996. Ten years on and figures from Dubai World highlight the success of trade through its eight free zones, which in 2006 alone grew by 8.9% to $52.7 billion. China is the leading source of imports at $4.9 billion, while Iran is the biggest re-export market at $2.6 billion. Impressively the Dubai Multi Commodities Centre made a maiden contribution of $1.7 billion, and the new DIFC added $6.4 million, a figure that should multiply many times over by the year 2015. Trade in the first half of 2008 grew by 50% against the same period in 2007.

The 29 million passengers using the Dubai International Airport in 2006 was testament enough to the success of Dubai in growing its tourism industry, and this figure is projected to hit 40 million in

2008. There will be an avalanche of new hotel openings in line for the next couple of years, including amazing luxury hotels linked to iconic global fashion designers like Versace and Armani. Even the world famous cruise liner the QEII is to be berthed in Dubai as a floating hotel. Coming up are the 60,000 rooms of the Al Bawadi project in Dubailand with the largest hotel in the world, the Asia-Asia with 6,500 rooms.

Emirates Airline has also upped its order for the new A380 superjumbo aircraft from 45 to 58 planes, and promises to order even more of the smaller planes, which will make it one of the largest long-haul airlines by 2015 with around 300 aircraft. Again, this ambition needs to be seen in context. A decade ago Emirates had 32 aircraft and when the airline's chairman Sheikh Ahmed bin Saeed Al Maktoum said he wanted to have a fleet of 100 planes people smiled and thought he must be daydreaming. In the summer of 2007 the fleet stood at 103 with new aircraft arriving every month from Airbus and Boeing. So what is happening is not a sudden phenomenon but the continuation of a careful organic growth strategy, and while Emirates is a fantastic business success story it is a long-running saga and not a flash in the pan. And who started the airline? Why none other than Sheikh Mohammed himself, who took the decision in 1985 when he was in charge of the Dubai airport and Gulf Air suddenly axed its services to Dubai leaving the emirate short of flights. It began with two leased aircraft and best global management practices and levered the economic advantages of Dubai.

The Dubailand theme park is the great hope for the future of local tourism. This is perhaps for Sheikh Mohammed what the Jebel Ali Free Zone was for his father. The investment totals are equally mind-blowing with $64 billion as one guestimate for the final cost of Dubailand, which is phased over 20 years, and will thus only be partly completed within the 2015 time horizon. The business objective is simply to provide a world-class theme park attraction to keep visitors to Dubai here for longer, and to get them to spend more. The main challenge is the fierce summer weather which may deter holidaymakers, but that does not stop them flocking to the emirate in the summer for cut-price hotel rates, and as much as possible of Dubailand will be indoors. Then there is the commercial challenge of producing a sufficient return on investment to justify the huge cost. To date, the sale of land associated with the 18 or more separate projects that comprise Dubailand, from the City of Arabia to Sports City, have provided the cash flow required for construction of the theme park attractions. The project is phased over two decades and so it could be expected to go through several business cycles before completion, though hopefully not providing a roller-coaster ride for investors.

It is inevitable that as a business hub for the region Dubai will go through business cycles, even though its heavily diversified economy provides some significant protection against the vicissitudes of the oil price. Emerging markets do tend to have some exaggerated swings up and down, and Dubai has seen this most recently in its spectacular stock market bust with the local bourse plunging two-thirds from its late 2005 peak. The real estate market is likely to go through a correction within the next few years, according to analysts from Standard Chartered Bank, UBS and EFG Hermes with a movement in prices to the downside.

What else is to be expected though? Dubai is presently the biggest construction site in the world with projects valued at towards $300 billion in hand, including the world's tallest building and two of the world's largest shopping malls. On the Dubai Marina site alone more than 100 towers are rising simultaneously. Some observers compare Dubai to Shanghai in 2000. The Chinese megalopolis had a spectacular real estate bust followed by a rapid recovery and another boom. Others see a recession in Western economies that will lower the oil price and leave Dubai to endure a violent downswing like Hong Kong post-1997, or a massive shakeout like

Singapore in the early 1980s. Or perhaps *The Economist* is right to argue that oil liquidity will ensure the boom deflates slowly like a tyre with a slow puncture.

Could it be that with all this economic expansion under way that the 2015 vision of Sheikh Mohammed will again actually understate the success to be achieved by the end of the new plan? It is certainly more than possible, even if the new planning period includes the real estate correction that many experts predict. For, over an eight year planning horizon a swing down before an even bigger swing upwards is always possible. It happened most recently in Shanghai.

However, any outside observer will acknowledge that Dubai has a long track record of investment into projects that appeared very ambitious at the time, but were later proven shrewd investments. Today, Dubai is investing in the Airbus A380 and the latest Boeing aircraft, a huge expansion of airport facilities including the new Maktoum International Airport, doubling its hotel capacity, the Dubailand theme park, the famous Palm Islands, hundreds of high-rise residential and commercial towers, free zones and the tallest building in the world, the Burj Dubai, and several of the world's biggest shopping malls.

Will there be a correction within this investment cycle? It would be far more astonishing if there was not. But long-term investors who stick with Dubai, and many of these investments are pure equity finance, will reap the rewards of a business vision that is a coherent whole. Dubai is really run as Dubai Inc. with Sheikh Mohammed as the charismatic, hands-on and visionary chief executive. And in any market downturn the government would likely be as proactive in its management as it has been in driving the investment boom forward. It would be the short-term investors with overstretched financial resources that would suffer most in a consolidation process. But that consolidation would only be strengthening of Dubai Inc. for the next leap forward.

Dubai's destiny is to become a bigger version of what it already is: a regional hub for trade, tourism and finance. This is exactly the constellation of business activities most likely to succeed in the future, and each requires enormous infrastructure support in terms of aviation and shipping, roads and bridges, a metro system, hotels, shopping malls, exhibition halls, offices and homes. It is enormously to Dubai's credit that the city has got on with building this necessary infrastructure during the first oil boom of the twenty-first century and not stalled while thinking about whether to take the risk. One of Sheikh Mohammed's favourite sayings is that sometimes the biggest risk is not taking a risk. In other words, procrastinate for too long and you miss the big opportunity. Dubai Inc. has gone all out to meet its destiny head on, and no other city in the Gulf States comes close in terms of expansion or planned expansion.

But if the best is yet to come, why did we sell out of our small dotcom enterprise? Why did we not choose to carry on growing with Dubai? It is only fair to bring the macro vision down to the micro level of AME Info, the main focus of this book. I think it is a matter of understanding that every dog has its day. As a small company we could only hope to hold our highly profitable position as the largest English language media in the Middle East for a short period. Success inevitably attracts competition. And while we levered the great business economics of Dubai, and opportunities like the DMC, to our advantage, global and local players with better capitalisation than our own had increasingly identified our success and wanted to copy, or like Emap, buy it. Therefore, it made good sense to sell out to Emap, the UK's second largest media company, while the going was good, and hence let them carry the business forward rather than do it ourselves.

In business life you need to know not only your strengths but also your limitations. How many companies grow from nothing only to end up squeezed by new competition and laid out in the next economic downturn? As a business journalist of more than two decades I had seen this sad prologue to success often enough to not to want to end up with the same fate. I was lucky enough to have partners of similar mind. We also hope and trust that in Emap plc AME Info has found a good home and will enjoy a successful and profitable future. One thing is quite certain – Emap is a long-term player with a strong and genuine commitment to the region. After all Emap's leading title the *Middle East Economic Digest* has just celebrated its fiftieth anniversary and AME Info is now a part of the same stable. Taking the longer view AME Info will surely ride out any ups and downs in the regional business cycle like MEED and keep a premium position.

From our perspective it has been a great experience to be a part of the Dubai Inc. success story as well as to follow its progress day by day, and an honour to be among the first dotcom millionaires to be created in the DMC. No doubt there will be more to come. Dubai remains a place where you can take an idea and have a go, with an excellent business infrastructure at your disposal for comparatively modest cost. But not everybody is a winner in a free enterprise system, and looking back not that many of the new ventures from 2000-2001 are still around. AME Info at least now has a new home with a strong global parent group which is committed to long term investment in the website. It will, with this backing, be able to see off whatever new local or global competition emerges in the future.